ASTEROIDS INTERPRETED

DAVE CAMPBELL

Copyright 2021 by American Federation of Astrologers, Inc. All rights reserved.

No part of this book may be reproduced or transcribed in any form or by any means, electronic or mechanical, including photocopying or recording or by any information storage and retrieval system without written permission from the author and publisher, except in the case of brief quotations embodied in critical reviews and articles. Requests and inquiries may be mailed to: American Federation of Astrologers, Inc., 6535 S. Rural Road, Tempe, AZ 85283.

ISBN-13: 978-0-86690-678-4

Editor: Celeste Nash-Weninger

Cover Design: Celeste Nash-Weninger

Published by:

American Federation of Astrologers, Inc.

6535 S. Rural Road

Tempe, AZ 85283

THIS BOOK IS DEDICATED TO ALL the past teachers and astrologers who have influenced my astrological career and training. Some special mentions are to Demetra George who started my journey into the asteroid realm, and the following but not totally inclusive, Joyce Jensen, Phillip Sedgwick, Jeff Green, Donna Cunningham, Martha Lang-Wescott, David and Fei Cochrane, Kim Falconer, Alex Miller, Mark Pottenger, Penny Thornton, Sy Scholfield,

Kris Brandt-Riske, Stephanie Clement, Madalyn Hillis Dinnen, just to name a few. I am deeply grateful to all the astrologers who helped shape my destiny.

CONTENTS

Introduction
Part 1: Ceres
    Ceres in the Signs   1
    Ceres in the Houses   7
    Ceres in Aspect   11
Part 2: Juno
    Juno in the Signs   35
    Juno in the Houses   40
    Juno in Aspect   45
Part 3: Pallas
    Pallas in the Signs   65
    Pallas in the Houses   71
    Pallas in Aspect   75
Part 4: Vesta
    Vesta in the Signs   95
    Vesta in the Houses   101
    Vesta in Aspect   105
Part 5: Chiron
    Chiron in the Signs   123
    Chiron in the Houses   129
    Chiron in Aspect   133

⚲

CERES

GODDESS OF THE GRAIN AND HARVEST

Goddess of the grain and harvest she rules over bread, food, sustenance and nutrition. Now considered a Dwarf Planet.

Key Words/themes:

Nurturing, unconditional love as a parent may have for a child. Care giving, grief loss and sorrow, separation. How did your mother nurture you physically with food? Represents a mother in our life along with the Moon. Eating habits, eating disorders such as anorexia or obesity. Working with food. Grief counselors, nannies. Abandonment issues. Custody battles. Pregnancy and child bearing. Cooks, chefs, food industry workers.

Other name: Demeter

Symbol: Wheat; Grains

CERES IN THE SIGNS

⚳

Ceres in Aries

You nurture by giving independence to others, and allowing them to show their strength. This was learned as it was how you were nurtured by your parents. When someone is down or weak you show you care by helping them become self-sufficient, and feeling better about themselves. You may tend to eat fast as Ceres has much to do with food and eating. You tend to be demonstrative to those you nurture by doing things for them. Career with this placement can be nurses, care givers, first responders,

Ceres in Taurus

For you, feeling loved may equate to feeling fed. You nurture by giving, and making others feel comfortable physically, warm, cozy, full, etc. This is also how you like to be nurtured and taken care of by others. Ceres in Taurus also likes to be outdoors in the earth, gardening, growing things or just taking care of the vegetation even cutting the grass. You enjoy the nicer things of quality that make you feel comfortable, clothes, home décor, or the finer foods. This placement is good for chefs, gardeners, agriculturists.

Ceres in Gemini

In order to feel loved, you need to be told so. The spoken word is so important to your self esteem, you want to hear it even if you feel it or know it – you **must** hear it. You nurture through your words. Dialog is more important to you than other ways of expressing your feelings. You may have been told you're so smart as a child that you identified being smart with being loved, so you feel the need to be in the know about many subjects. Your parents may have been very talkative and interested in many different subjects. This makes you a great communicator, teaching is a great area for you.

Ceres in Cancer

Nurturing and caretaking are second nature to you. You feel deeply, and show it through taking care of others, feeding them, and helping with their daily needs. You have a very strong relationship with your mother, as she was very comforting to be around. Food is a way to your heart, as you associate food with comfort and nurturing, take care not to let this become a problem. This placement is good for those in food service, chefs, caregivers, and nannies.

Ceres in Leo

Your parents were really proud of you. This instilled a strong confidence in you. You nurture by demonstrating pride in the object of your desires and showing gratitude and appreciation. You can also show caring by helping them develop their own creativity and greatness. You like to be nurtured by hearing how great and wonderful you are as well. You could work in a position as a master chef, working in the creative arts, or coaching, especially with children.

Ceres in Virgo

You were taught that to be loved you needed to be helpful, doing something for others; and even to do things 'right way', was necessary. As a result you nurture by doing things for the affection of others. This is not a bad thing, as you are doing it because you want to be of service to them and to show your love. You enjoy doing the tasks that are shared in a household. You have high standards and can even be a perfectionist, which is okay as long as it's kept healthy and doesn't become conditional to love. Working in the food service industry is great for this placement, as well as the health care industry.

Ceres in Libra

In order for you to feel nurtured you need to be treated with kindness, and harmony. You need cooperation to feel whole and loved, so the need to be in a relationship is strong with this placement. You are the peacemaker and that is how you nurture others, through kindness, sympathy, fairness and understanding. You're also very romantic towards those for whom you have affection. You love receiving and sending flowers to show your affection. This placement is great for matchmakers, relationship counselors, and those in the justice fields.

Ceres in Scorpio

You feel deeply and very intensely, and in order to feel nurtured you need this same intensity reflected back to you; deep intense emotion – passion. You go to the soul level, leaving nothing unturned. Sex is a very strong way for you to feel nurtured, and one way you show that you're nurturing and caring. You feel a deep bond with those you care about. You need to be careful not to smother with love, as Ceres here can be a little controlling. Ceres here is good for hospice workers and grief counselors.

Ceres in Sagittarius

You nurture people with your generosity cheerfulness and encouragement. Giving them the optimism and openness they need. You aim to inspire them and make them feel like they are 'it'. Your honest disposition and behavior is also a gift for them to know your devotion to them. All of these things are exactly what you need in order to feel cared for. Higher education and philosophy also helps you feel nurtured; learning more, it feeds your soul. Your parents allowed you to expand beyond the philosophies or beliefs of the family tradition.

Ceres in Capricorn

You feel nurtured and cared for when you feel safe and secure, when there is structure, and you're provided for. This is how you were taken care of by your parents, they were strong providers, giving you shelter and food on the table. This is now how you nurture, by providing and making those you care about feel safe, secure and provided for. Many with this placement may make a career out of the Ceres talents; cooking, care taking, nursing.

Ceres in Aquarius

You may have received what others would call unconventional nurturing. The relationship you have with your parents may not have seemed "normal", and may have seemed more like a friendship more than a parent-child relationship. This taught you to nurture by being independent not clingy or mushy but unique, by being a friend and encouraging individuality. You nurture by being friends with those you love, you may have unconventional ways of showing your love. You may feel loved by being part of the group/family unit by giving your unique talents, and contributions to the family.

Ceres in Pisces

Nurturing is second nature to you, as you are an empath.

You feel others deeply, which is how you nurture, with lots of deep sympathetic emotion. You are a rescuer and care giver. This can lead to co-dependency so take care not to give too much of yourself that you lose your own identity. Ceres in Pisces is very devoted to those they care about. Positions as a caretaker, social worker, or some creative outlet is good for you. You often feel like others are your soul mate, you are feeling the connection from past lives.

CERES IN THE HOUSES

⚳

Ceres in the first house

You are the personification of Ceres; care giver, nurturer, parental, responsible. You have interest in subjects related to Ceres: agriculture, gardening, caretaking, food and nutrition. You may be the one to nurture yourself, as well as others. You love helping and providing for others, you may be seen as the "parent" or responsible one.

Ceres in the Second House

You may make money in areas ruled by Ceres; food service, cook-chef, bartender, nanny care giver, grief counselor, gardener. Providing food and shelter helps you feel nurtured and is how you nurture others. You value being able to help others. Shopping for things gives you lots of comfort, be careful not to let spending get out of hand, as objects do not translate to happiness – as in hoarding.

Ceres in the Third House

This placement may mean an older sibling was part of the parenting, and nurturing picture in your life. Learning and early schooling brings you much nourishment and makes you feel nurtured. You may teach as this is an outlet for you to nurture others. Words make you feel comfort.

Ceres in the Fourth House

Being a parent and care giver is highly important to you. There is a strong love of family and family life being very close together. There was a strong bond between mother and you as a child. Your home life was very comforting, and nurturing. It may be hard for you to leave the nest when it is time.

Ceres in the Fifth House

This placement shows lots of domestic talents and creativity in Ceres related fields; food, caretaking, child rearing, gardening, and agriculture. You may even become a professional in one of those areas. In your love affairs you may be attracted to the Ceres archetype; provider, parental, caretaking, nurturing, someone you feel you could start a family with, the mother or father of your children.

Ceres in the Sixth house

This placement is strong for Ceres, as this house resonates with the archetype. You are very particular about the foods you eat, and may be very sensitive to certain foods, diet is important to you. You love taking care of small animals, and pets, and may have an interest in pursuing this as a career, – veterinarian etc. Another avenue for your vocation is the health care industry.

Ceres in the seventh house

Your spouse may be in the caretaking, or hospitality industry. Your partner will be very kind, with a care giving type of personality. You have a very strong bond with your partner, the give and take in nurturing most likely works in both directions.

Ceres in the Eighth House

In order to feel cared for you need a very cathartic and deep bond with your partner. Sexuality may be a way for you to feel nurtured, and the way you nurture. You may actually have to care for the dying, as in hospice work, or with very ill people. You may have experienced heavy grief in your life as someone close to you has passed to the other side, making you feel very deeply. This is a great placement for a grief counselor, or someone who does the care giving for the survivors of death.

Ceres in the Ninth House

Your taste in foods may be on the exotic side, foreign foods from many different cultures and countries excite your palate. Cultivating your higher mind is nurturing for you. Exploring new ideas, and ways to grow gives you the comfort needed. You encourage others to learn and grow, it gives you joy and happiness to see someone grow. Getting a work promotion and a transfer to another location is a source of joy and happiness for you, and travel is a source of nurturing for your soul. Your mother may have been from a different background or you may have had a nanny from another country or culture. You feel comfortable being "on the road".

Ceres in the Tenth house

Success in the workplace makes you feel nurtured. You may feel" at home" in the workplace, or office. This placement is great for cooks, bakers, chefs, bartenders, and the service industry, nannies, maids, as well as in landscaping, agriculture, and farming. Your parent(s) may have been very career oriented sending the message that they cared by working for your well-being.

Ceres in the Eleventh house

You seek nurturing in an unusual way, not too close or

smothering, but by being a friend, and showing you care. Your mother may have seemed more like a friend than a mother. You are very close to your friends and may see them more as family. You may "mother your friends. This placement can indicate step-parenting. You see the world as your mother in a larger scale, or scheme of things. Many with this placement are environmentalists, caring for the earth.

Ceres in the Twelfth House

This placement is great for working as a caretaker in the twelfth house areas, such as, hospitals for nursing, or cafeteria work in prisons, and large corporations. Your work is usually behind the scenes, not in the public eye. Ceres in the twelfth indicates a empathic personality, one who subconsciously feels, the needs of others. This can be an issue, if you don't look after your own nurturing needs. You may have a hard time figuring out what your caretaking needs are, as they are subconscious for you. Look deep within to insure that you take care of yourself, before co-dependency sets in.

CERES IN ASPECT

⚳

Ceres Conjunction Sun

You are the nurturer and care giver in life and will be the surrogate parent for those around you. Domestic roles are perfect for you. Your aptitude in vocation centers on the following areas: food service, chef, care giver to children or elderly, hospice work, nanny, gardener, farmer, and agriculture. Family is of huge importance to you. You tend to be a hardworking person.

Ceres sextile Sun

You are very loving. You love family life, and enjoy being the care giver and parent to others. You may have had to take care of the family early on, cooking, and looking after your younger siblings. This made you more mature and parent-like in your youth. Hospitality industries would be great for you such as hotelier, cook at a restaurant, or working with plants, and farming as you have talents in these areas. You are a natural green thumb in the garden.

Ceres Square Sun

There may be issues with the care giving demands of life such as parenting, taking care of others and doing what you want in life. Sometimes marrying and having children at a young age can create this, or being the older sibling who has to take care of the younger brothers and sisters instead of going out with friends, is an early outcome of this aspect. Your mother may have been overly concerned for your well-being. She may have "killed you with kindness", such as overfeeding you, or "smothering you with love", resulting in issues with being cared for.

Ceres Trine Sun

You seem to have a natural talent for working with plants, food, and care giving of others, children or the elderly. You enjoy cooking for others, making them feel comfortable and cared for. This is a great trait you possess. Talents include food service, chef, gardener, or working with agriculture and farming. You have a natural green thumb. Your parents taught you well and took care of your innermost needs while growing up. Nutrition and food are important to you, make sure to keep proper balance as with this aspect it can be easy to overindulge in food.

Ceres Opposition Sun

You may have a hard time trusting those that care for you and nurture you. Rejection issues from early childhood as a result of the nurturing you did or did not receive from your mother. It may seem hard for you to get close to others as you have abandonment issues in relationships and this creates the separation and loss issues within you. Allow others to take care of you, put the trust back into your relationships. You have difficulty showing caring and nurturing towards others, especially your significant other.

Ceres Conjunction Moon

To feel emotionally secure you must feel a strong connection to those you care about. You have a strong need to feel cared for. You are especially good at nurturing those you care for, making sure they have all the comforts they need, food, shelter, a nice bed, and a nice home. You have the mother archetype whether male or female, you are a care giver. Food can be a way you show your affection for others, and was one way you were shown that you were loved. This can be a problem, as you may identify food as equating to love, this can create a weight problem if not kept in proper balance.

Ceres sextile Moon

You are a selfless giver, loving to show affection for those around you at any time. You have a great imagination in the cooking department, creative food dishes full of color, making your plates look like art. This is a good aspect for working with vegetation, planting and growing. Your warm personality and presence makes others feel welcome. You have an aura of comfort, and safety.

Ceres Square Moon

You and your Mother did not always see eye to eye with each other. Her care giving style did not go over well with your emotional needs. She may have been overcommitted with other children or a career that needed her attention, which took away from you and the nurturing you needed. This may have created issues of rejection, loneliness, and isolation. Work towards integrating your emotional needs, speak up about them. Do not waste your time on people who are not worthy of giving your nurturing to, if they are not giving you emotionally what you need. This aspect can create emotional eating when in a bad mood, which can cause weight gain. Review your ideas about food, and see how they relate to overeating. This aspect has made you a very strong person.

Ceres Trine Moon

You are a comforting person to be around, as your always making sure everyone is being taken care of. This position works well with hostess work, restaurant work, and care giving and service industry people. There is talent around food preparation and cooking as well as growing vegetables or fruits. There is harmony in your emotional life and your home life. Mother was a strong influence on your life. Your home life is very positive.

Ceres Opposition Moon

You have a difficult time trusting your feelings when someone tries to take care of you, or shows you affection. Relationships can be difficult as your nurturing style and their emotional needs are not matching up. You have strong feelings of rejection, or conditional love, based on what you learned from mother. She may have been too busy to nurture you properly, thus you did not learn how to nurture others. This is something you need to work on to integrate emotional fulfillment with your nurturing and care giving style.

Ceres Conjunction Mercury

Your communication is very harmonious, and nurturing to others. You have a pleasing voice, and communication style that is nurturing. You use words that are very thoughtful and therapeutic to others. You like showing your affection with words.

Ceres sextile Mercury

Your ideas and the thoughts you convey are well received by others. Many people benefit from hearing you speak and are inspired by your voice and your words. Opportunities exist for you to use your communication spoken or written, as this is a great aspect for writers. You may write about any subject, however you can excel in subjects such as: domestic life, care giving, gardening, healing, nurturing, and caring for the grieving.

Ceres Square Mercury

Communication was not encouraged while growing up. This may make you feel inadequate in your speaking and writing skills. There may have been conditioning with hard words etc. There may have been circumstances that prevented much communication from mother, and the nurturing that brings. Learn to communicate with words that are healing, and encouraging. Your self-esteem is wrapped up in communications, and "what people will say". Don't be harsh with yourself. A sibling may have taken time away from you with your mother, work on healing this and integrating it into your life.

Ceres Trine Mercury

You have the gift of communication on an emotional level, you understand what people are feeling without saying. This may translate to animal communication, or subliminal understanding of situations. You would work well with autistic children as you can understand them on another level that others cannot. Your words are received well from others work in radio would be a great avenue for you. Writing is a great outlet for you. You understand how things grow in plant world, and have a talent for communicating with plants.

Ceres Opposition Mercury

Communication may be difficult in relationships, as it is hard for you to express your nurturing side and your needs. You find it hard to tell people you care about them. You may expect the other half to just know what your needs are, causing friction and tension when they don't come through. It feels awkward when you express your affections and feelings, as well as when someone does the same towards you.

Ceres Conjunction Venus

Love and nurturing combine, this says mother loved you and nurtured you as a child. This can equate to looking for a mate who is like "mom", a care giver, and nurturer. This aspect gives talents in cooking, especially baking and decorating with sweets, and pastries. You may have been taught that to be nurtured you need to be attractive. You have a sweet tooth for desserts of all kinds.

Ceres Sextile Venus

This aspect is great for your relationships, in that you attract harmonious and nurturing and care giving partners. There was great expression of love and care giving from mother that creates the vibration of harmony in your relationships. There is talent with domestic life, decorating, cooking, baking and food preparation. You work well with plants and would be great at arranging flowers. Florists and landscaping are favored with this aspect.

Ceres square Venus

Ceres square Venus shows complexes with your self-worth and your feeling attractive. You may have been conditioned to believe that beauty equals love. You may feel undesirable and sexually unattractive if you don't look a certain way. Food can be an issue especially sugary sweets. This can lead to food complexes such as bulimia and anorexia nervosa.

Ceres Trine Venus

This aspect gives affection and care giving in your relationships. This shows a nurturing and care-giving marriage is likely. There is great talent in food presentation, as you can prepare a beautiful dish or spread. This is also a strong fertility aspect, in both sexes, showing possibilities of many children. This aspect favors great cooks, chefs, landscaping design, florists and decorators.

Ceres Opposition Venus

Relationships may be challenging in that it is hard for

you to give and receive affection and nurturing. Parents may not have shown enough nurturing or care giving in your childhood, as they may have been too busy with their own lives and you did not develop a very nurturing and affectionate personality. There can be issues with food, especially sugary foods, and your self-image or self-esteem. This can lead to eating disorders, overweight, anorexia nervosa, bulimia etc. You can integrate the inadequate feelings by being more demonstrative with your nurturing and care giving.

Ceres Conjunction Mars

Ceres Conjunction Mars shows strong demonstrative cargiving style. You act on things rather quickly to show that you care. By doing the chores, cleaning the house and doing things is how you show your affection, and nurturing. You may have been nurtured or "mothered" by mostly male figures as a child, i.e.: from your father.

Ceres sextile Mars

You love to show that you care by helping others, and doing things for them. You are a very productive individual with long lasting endurance for getting things done. Ceres sextile Mars favors people who work hard, especially in food production such as butchers, farmers and those in the fields.

Ceres square Mars

This aspect shows a conflict of independence versus nurturing, and care giving. There may have been a smothering parent that wouldn't give you the chance to do things on your own, making you rebel in the process, and getting angry over the situation. This can translate to family arguments at the dinner table. Food issues can be a problem with this aspect as well, high stomach acids, acid reflux, food allergies such as gluten are a possibility.

Ceres Trine Mars

You have a strong confident nature, and are not afraid to show your affections towards others. This can manifest as a care taker in emergency situations, such as a nurse, first responder, delivering a baby etc., all exemplify Ceres trine Mars. You are chivalrous in doing things for your mate. You have talents with taking action on the home scene, gardening, doing the domestic chores, and you're even talented in the kitchen.

Ceres Opposition Mars

Relationships may be a little difficult in the care giving and nurturing department. There can be anger toward the one who shows you care and concern. This relates to smothering of love from a parent, most likely the mother who didn't give you a chance to assert yourself or be independent. You may take any care giving as a form of control. Issues with foods can be a problem; upset stomach, ulcers, and acid reflux can be problematic.

Ceres Conjunction Jupiter

You have a warm and expressive nurturing style, making people feel good inside. This is the type of nurturing you received as well. There may be talent in growing things in the garden, cooking in the kitchen or with care giving and hosting. For you nurturing means expansion and growth in education and understanding of the bigger picture. There can be pitfalls of too much of a good thing, especially around food as you like a smorgasbord of different foods.

Ceres Sextile Jupiter

You bring new ideas to a couple different areas – in the kitchen for one, with food, and cooking; also, in the garden with growing things or even as a business in agriculture. You have lots of new ideas around care giving, nurturing, food and nutrition. You have a jovial personality, making others feel warm and comforted inside with your wisdom and your care giving style.

Ceres Square Jupiter

There may be challenges with food and eating, watching to be cautious of over eating will be a challenge. There can be issues with foreign foods or rich foods that don't agree with you. Over- nurturing of others, like smothering or killing with kindness may be something you have to watch, as it is the way you too were nurtured in your childhood.

Ceres Trine Jupiter

Ceres trine Jupiter shows that you had a very nurturing mother who showed you the ropes in a couple areas, one being in the kitchen with food preparation and cooking, the other may have been in the garden, growing things and harvesting them. You could be a master chef with this aspect or make a living through vegetation, and agriculture. You have a knack for making others feel welcome, and cared for in personal life as well as professional. Care giving to others is also a talent you possess. This aspect gives you a friendly warm disposition.

Ceres Opposition Jupiter

There may be disagreements with your significant other(s), you may have differing beliefs and nurturing styles. This stems from having a different belief system or religion than your mother has, or had. Issues over food and eating may come into play as well, even over whether prayer is included or not at the dinner table. There can be times of over indulgence to times of lack or very nutritional diet. Your Mother may have had to travel for work at times, being absent off and on, and with this distance grandparents may have had to take over for a while.

Ceres Conjunction Saturn

You may be too busy to remember to eat. You will have to make sure you don't get over busy taking care of everyone else's needs and neglect your own. Care giving may seem like a duty to you, and it may have seemed that is the way mother nurtured you, by simply taking care of you, feeding etc. There may not have been warm fuzzy feelings about it just matter of fact care giving. You could make good use of this energy by making a career out of either care giving, or nurturing as a business.

Ceres Sextile Saturn

Ceres sextile Saturn shows that you make good use of your time especially where duties involving care giving are needed. You bring new methods to giving care to others, and even new ways of cooking or organizing the kitchen. You bring care giving to a practical level, very thoughtful of the needs of others, you respond by doing just what needs to be done.

Ceres Square Saturn

You may have issues with your food intake, and nutrition, keeping your vitamin levels normal. Be sure that your eating habits are well balanced and full of rich food sources high in vitamins and minerals, as there can be lack with this aspect. You may literally not like eating. Food allergies to gluten may manifest. You may have too much on your plate with the high priorities of your work-life's demands versus the daily needs of care giving, food and nutrition. You have to juggle taking care of family versus your work-life and boss' demands. Your mother may have had so many responsibilities and duties that it was hard to nurture you properly or only as time allowed.

Ceres Trine Saturn

You are a very busy person with many responsibilities that you seem to handle well keeping the balance with domestic duties, such as cooking, cleaning and family obligations, to holding down a full time job. You have mastered the two worlds, and been responsible in both directions. This came from a well-balanced upbringing where you had to do your part of the household chores. Career and family life should be successful for you on both fronts. Careers in the domestic areas would also be good for you such as care taking, food service, or hotelier would all be suitable.

Ceres Opposition Saturn

This aspect can show there may have been a separation from a father figure literally or maybe he was overly involved with work, and did not have much time to do his part of the nurturing. This can also indicate a custody battle in which your father only got to see you part time. This can manifest in issues of taking responsibility with household duties, cooking, cleaning and responsibility in general. Balancing both career and home life can be the ongoing challenge.

Ceres Conjunction Uranus

Your upbringing was most likely anything but conventional and boring. There were plenty of adventures and unusual events taking place. Non-traditional is a good way to put your early years. Mother may have been into new age thought or a trendy mom that was innovative – she could have been an astrologer. New and exciting foods exhilarate you, and you do have strange tastes in food, from the exotic to the untried. Your nurturing style is innovative and you like to put a little of the unexpected into your daily routine. You are not the clingy overly mothering type, you're the type to show nurturing by allowing independence, and encouraging others in that direction.

Ceres Sextile Uranus

Your mother was a great friend to you, showing a closer than usual relationship but also being almost more friends than mother-child. You do well helping and nurturing strangers and friends, much in the same way you do with your own family, and loved ones. It may not be always conventional, where everyone is off doing their own thing at dinner time, but the love is still there. Your individuality was encouraged through nurturing, embracing the uniqueness of being yourself, and encouraging that in others. You enjoy making new and fun foods that would challenge the best chefs.

Ceres Square Uranus

There may have been a broken home or an early divorce in your upbringing, that may have even caused you to be a little rebellious, especially toward your mother. At the very least your upbringing was not the usual and may have been a little stressful or erratic at times. This can carry over into relationship issues where it is hard for you to get "close" to others on a deep and feeling level. There is a strong need to regain balance in relationships while being able to be yourself and keep your independence. Your relationship with mom improves as you get older, as there may have been too much going on for her to be as close as she liked at the time.

Ceres Trine Uranus

You have a good time trying new foods, the more exotic the better. You care for and nurture people in a friendly although unattached way. You could even have a more non-conditional type nurturing style. Your friends may be on the unusual side, you love to nurture them, and take good care of the "odd" ones, as you see their potential in life. This is a great placement for adopting children that have been through trauma.

Ceres Opposition Uranus

It may be difficult for you to get close to others on a personal level. This stems from a rebellious relationship with your mother at a young age. You may have been rebelling and trying to keep her away from you as you are highly unique and very different from her. There may have been separation from mother in your early life, she may have been too busy, or stressed with other pressing issues and you felt neglected because of this. There is still love there, it's just more difficult to express feelings and to connect with this aspect. Learning to integrate the uniqueness of everyone, even though extremely different from you, and still caring for them will assist you in your life. You may take care of others with whom you have no relationship on a personal level.

Ceres Conjunction Neptune

You may be a very spiritual and compassionate individual as you love unconditionally and without any thought of what's in it for me. You are very sensitive and psychic in feeling what others needs are, for nurturing and care giving. You are a natural empath. This can be a blessing or sometimes feel like a curse, as you feel all the emotions of people around you without any boundaries. This can be too much to handle until you learn to put up boundaries to shield from this constant bombardment. This does however make you great at the healing professions like counselor, nurse, healer, psychic, psychologist. One other negative potential here is if you do not learn to shield and protect yourself you may turn to an escape route, like drugs or alcohol, to hide from all the overwhelming emotions.

Ceres Sextile Neptune

People see you as such a nice person who always is thoughtful and knows just what it is they need to make them feel comfortable. You are a selfless giver with great sympathy for those you love and care for. You can be highly creative with food and are instinctually guided to good nutrition, knowing what your body needs. You just have to remember to listen to it as it can also be easy to choose the fancy, and fun foods. This is a great aspect for aromatherapy, utilizing it and being an aroma therapist; it would also favor anesthesiologists.

Ceres Square Neptune

You may have had issues with Mother in your upbringing, as you were confused, there was a lot going on that was being kept from you. There may have been addiction issues in the family that were hidden. It may have been food addiction or some other type of addiction including religious addiction. This has a high potential for creating co-dependency issues with you, and in the family. Learn to say what you mean, and take care of yourself first then others. Be sure not to put yourself on the back burner, in relationships. You may have food allergies especially to gluten with this aspect. Food addiction as an escape can also be an issue to deal with.

Ceres Trine Neptune

You're a very compassionate person who gives of yourself freely, without expectation of reward. Unconditional love is easy for you. This aspect is good for healers and care givers. You have a natural intuition of what others needs are without having to be told. You are a natural caretaker. Your creative and artistic side may include food presentation and design. This aspect favors charity work, and also the healing arts, nursing, anesthesiologists and other like professions.

Ceres Opposition Neptune

You are very compassionate and sympathetic to others instinctually. This means you're an empath. You will need to learn how to put up boundaries, as this aspect can produce co-dependent issues that need to be resolved. Be sure to give to others that deserve your care giving skills, and make sure you're not trying to rescue and save everyone, while sacrificing yourself. There can be many lessons causing distrust, and disappointment as many may have lied to you or deceived you into care giving for them. Trust yourself. You are very giving it's just that you need to keep boundaries in check to prevent from going overboard.

Ceres Conjunction Pluto

You have a very deep connection with those you care about, intense is a good word. Be careful to not be to controlling or over protective which this aspect can imply. You feel on a soul level which many people may not understand or relate to. When others are having a tough time or in heavy grief, you are there to help and face the situation head on where others might have left. You have had to deal with many endings in relationships in life from an early age, which would make you an excellent grief counselor, therapist, or psychologist. Abandonment issues may be an issue you have to learn to cope with, stemming from your mother, as she was very emotional as well. There may be issues with endings in relationships leading to obsession. Food and eating can be an obsession, whether too much or too little.

Ceres Sextile Pluto

You have a very deep feeling and nurturing nature. You sense what the deep needs are for others, and respond almost as if subconsciously. Although you have gone through many losses and endings you have responded well with the new beginnings that always follow endings, transforming your life with the new opportunities that present themselves. You have a sense of how to assist others with their grief and abandonment issues, which can even be a career aptitude or opportunity.

Ceres Square Pluto

There may have been many issues with power and control in your life, and may have stemmed from your relationship with your mother. She may have been a bit too controlling or she may have "killed you with kindness" or literally manipulated you with emotional blackmail. Life's transitions may seem overwhelming to you life and death issues are especially challenging. Your nurturing style is very intense and deep to the core, many may have a hard time understanding your intensity: to try to lighten up in this area, realizing you need to surrender to be free. Depression can be a result of taking life too seriously.

Eating and food may be a challenge; often this aspect means anything from anorexia, to overeating, to extreme cleansing. Make sure to keep fiber in your diet, and to eat well balanced meals. You're eating habits are tied to your emotions especially when there in grief sorrow and loss in your life.

Ceres Trine Pluto

You have very strong and deep feelings about those you care about. This is a good thing, and you are able to handle the deep feelings well. You are an extreme caregiver in that nothing you do is superficial, or in any way fake. You would work well in hospice or in a critical care department in a hospital. You can handle the most intense and even at times horrific situations with ease and concern for those involved. You would do well in the psychological fields, nursing, emergency responder etc. You are good at helping others with their life/death/ transition periods. You have a good balance in your diet, regular cleansing from time to time is helpful, ensuring fiber is a big part of your diet.

Ceres Opposition Pluto

There may be many power and control themes in your relationships, ending up with emotional blackmail as part of the relationship dynamics. "You would do this for me if you loved me" is one of the most toxic statements you will ever hear, this is emotional blackmail. You may have experienced great loss of people you have loved in life resulting in emotional reactions to loss that may seem insurmountable. Abandonment issues may be something you need to work on, by realizing that in the big picture this is only a small amount of time in eternity: keep perspective on many lifetimes. This will help ease the severity of the feelings.

Eating may be difficult for you when you feel grief or loss, this is normal. It is not normal if it stretches out over a period of time. If there are eating or food issues you need to examine the area of grief, loss and separation anxiety.

Ceres Conjunction Juno

You have or will have a good relationship with your spouse as far as care giving, and nurturing are concerned. He or she will be a great care giver with you, and you will also be a great nurturer for him/her. This can relate to a career or life path as a house wife or stay at home dad, or as a care giver.

Ceres Sextile Juno

You have a great relationship with your spouse or other half. There is equal time with each other as far as care giving and parenting roles, the balance seems to be fair. Eating is an enjoyable pastime with your partner. To share loving and fulfilling experiences with each other is indicated with this aspect. You enjoy taking care of each other.

Ceres Square Juno

Your significant relationship with your spouse or other half is off balance. There may be arguments over who has the house chores this week versus last week, the cooking roles are included in this. Parenting issues may be a challenge if you believe in different ways of raising, and disciplining a child. You and your other half may have huge differences in food tastes. There is challenge in all these areas.

Ceres Trine Juno

You have a lot in common with your other half, and the roles between the two of you seem to be complimentary. There most likely is a balance between you in your domestic roles, they seem to work for you. Eating habits and foods are shared and enjoyed with each other.

Ceres Opposition Juno

You may have conflicting ideas about your role as a care giver, versus your role as a partner, husband or wife depending. You may think that the tradition is not what you want in your own life. This also indicates that your spouse and you could have vastly different ideas of roles within the relationship as in the domestic issues, cooking etc. Your partner may not be nurturing at all.

Ceres Conjunction Pallas

Your parents nurtured you through education and making sure you had the skills, needed for success. This is how you nurture others as well. By keeping your intellect sharp, and well rounded, you keep nurturing yourself through education. Your mother was likely a career woman.

Ceres Sextile Pallas

You have a good sense of how to serve others, to make them feel comfortable and nurtured almost in a calculated way. You plan how to assist others and mother them. You may not be the emotional type, but more of an intellectual type of nurturer, which would make you good at helping those in need in the public, with whom you have no attachment.

Ceres Square Pallas

Pallas was not the type to need or want too much nurturing; this can put one at odds with the mother. There may be issues of trying to please the father, which creates issues with mother. There can be conflicts with parenting versus working, and in this day and age it is a very common for both sexes. There can be blocks to nurturing as it being seen as a smothering or a weakness within your psyche and something you need to integrate for positive outcomes in your affairs.

Ceres Trine Pallas

You have a good sense of how to nurture others in a most positive way without smothering them or making them feel needy. You have a way of empowering them through your care giving and nurturing skills. There was great pride from your mother in your intellectual skills as that is the way she nurtured you by making sure you could take care of yourself through your knowledge.

Ceres Opposition Pallas

There will be times in your relationships where you're the nurturer and the one doing the care giving, and times when you have to be the logical, rational and strategic one who appears to be impersonal, and extremely independent. This may be a theme in which you attract both of these archetypes at different times, and you must switch roles based on which of these you are being at the time.

Ceres Conjunction Vesta

You are a very dedicated person toward those to whom you are committed Devotion is second nature to you as you are very devoted to family and a real care-giver to those you love. You may even be nurtured through your occupation, your vision of life, or your religious or spiritual life.

Ceres Sextile Vesta

You're a very devoted person to your family and anything you commit your life to – person or cause. Giving service and dedication is your natural state of being. You may even find a career that deals with caretaking for elderly or children, or food service, both may be the case.

Ceres Square Vesta

You may have challenges with devotion to family and care giving versus work and career, to which you have dedicated yourself, as well. It may be a spiritual calling that is in conflict with your family or care giving obligations.

Ceres Trine Vesta

A career that includes your nurturing style would be the perfect place to show your talents in both dedication and service. Careers in catering, caring for the elderly, and planning their meals, or with children, such as a devoted nanny or care giver.

Ceres Opposition Vesta

Conflicts with relationships of care giving and nurturing versus career and work obligations. These obligations conflict with your time at home, especially around meal time, such as never being home for dinner or having to leave before breakfast, as there is no time for it. Integrating the two into your personal life and with your partnerships will help you out immensely.

Ceres Conjunction ASC

You are the personification of the care giver and nurturer in your life role. You will always be called upon to help, nurture and be the care taker of others: children, spouses, family, and friends included. People think of you as the one who will be depended on to make dinner, or breakfast, the mother role whether your male or female.

Ceres Sextile ASC

You have a great caring and nurturing feel about you, which others notice. This is a natural part of your persona. You most likely know your way around cooking and the kitchen, and the duties of domestic life. People see you as the care giver.

Ceres Square ASC

You may find it difficult to express your nurturing side, as it is uncomfortable for you because your parents were not this way, which led you to express nurturing through your work, much like your busy parents. Learning to integrate the nurturing in your personal life with a personal touch is the key for you.

Ceres Trine ASC

People see you as the caretaker and that is a big part of your role. Your talents on the domestic scene include cooking, gardening, and caring for others. This can translate into a career model, as this comes naturally to you. Careers as a chef, short order cook, caretaker, gardener or agriculturist suit you well.

Ceres Opposition ASC

You're likely to attract relationships that are very nurturing to people, as well as the care giver type. They will be good with the domestic life, cooking, and taking care of you and others. This may be something you need to integrate into your own persona, so learning from your partnerships will teach you how to express this part of yourself.

Ceres Conjunction MC

This is the placement of an executive in the area of Ceres rulerships. Care-taking of children or the elderly, or as a nanny, butler, chef or cook, or in the agriculture fields, as well as gardener. In your role at work you are the chief care giver, and you nurture those around and under you. If you're in a leadership role you are seen as the caring boss.

Ceres Sextile MC

You have special talent and opportunities in the realm of caretaking and nurturing as a business or career. This includes food service, cooking, chef, and care giving careers, as well as grief counselors, care givers; nanny, or butlers, and then the agricultural fields to gardening.

Ceres Square MC

There may be challenges in the workplace over issues of not feeling nurtured or taken care of. There can be issues with food, with not eating at work, or being too difficult to eat at work. Your parents food tastes were completely opposite yours, or not what you would like. You may not have felt nurtured or cared for in the way you needed to be by your parents; it may have been that they were too busy with work or with others to give you the attention you needed.

Ceres Trine MC

This is the aspect of the caretaker, chef, and the supportive mother, you have talents in all these areas, likely with one being stronger than the other. You have great luck with nurturing, and being very creative in these areas, like an artistic baker or chef. You can make money with these skills and talents. You make food preparation "look easy" as they say. This also shows your mother was a positive influence in your career choice.

Ceres Opposition MC

This placement shows there may be some odds where work versus home life is concerned. Do you feel you need to be at home to be nurtured or nurturing? Do you tend to withhold food or self care while at work? Likely your mother was a strong influence in the family, and you may even have some career goals, and/or issues as a result of this. This is something you can observe yourself to analyze and see which one it was. This also indicates there may be difficulties balancing self care due to over-working – as in workaholic tendencies.

Ceres Conjunction Chiron

This combination shows healing with food as nurturing. You may have strong interest in health foods, nutrition, and the effects of food. This may be due to some issue you had with food, such as allergies, food complexes, gluten sensitivities etc.

Ceres Sextile Chiron

You have a natural capacity to help others through nurturing and food. You are a natural, and this placement can indicate a master chef. Gardening and food preparation can be a strong talent and interest to you. Nurturing may even be a career for you as it is a natural talent that can easily translate to a career in the field. Care giving, food service, day care, grief counseling are just some of the possibilities with this placement.

Ceres Square Chiron

There may be health issues with food, wheat, gluten, etc.

Grief can also be an issue that needs to be resolved in your life. You are a natural care giver, the challenge around this may be a large challenge for you but it is one you must conquer.

Ceres Trine Chiron

You are a natural healer, and care giver, it comes easily and is second nature to you. You are the one who takes care of those in need. When others need help and healing they come to you. This can lead to a career in the healing fields, traditional or alternative. Careers can also include being master chef, caretaker, nutritionist, and horticulturist.

Ceres Opposition Chiron

Issues in your relationships may be around smothering, caring too much, co-dependency. Be sure to take care of yourself first, then others. You may have to be a care giver to the one you're with, or vice-versa. Sometimes the roles switch seemingly like clockwork. Learn to integrate your healing needs and not to project them onto others, or partnerships. Food challenges or allergies can be a result of this aspect.

JUNO

GODDESS OF MARRIAGE

As Goddess of Marriage, she keeps vows sacred, and honored. She was the wife of Zeus/Jupiter.

Key Words/Themes: Marriage partner (male or female) your ability to be in a marriage, or committed relationship. Fidelity, commitment, contract, significant other, dedicated and devoted partner. Power and control, shared resources-money. Juno describes your marriage by house and sign. Rituals and ceremonies, quarrels, jealousy, revengeful when wronged. Co-ruler or vice-president.

Other name: Hera

Totem: Peacock

JUNO IN THE SIGNS

Juno in Aries

Relationship needs center on independence for both you and your mate. You must be able to keep your independence within a committed relationship. Your partner will be as strong and independent as are you. You also need a mate who is outgoing, and energetic, there may even be a sense of competition between the two of you that you both rather enjoy. It is best to encourage each other to do your personal best and be a healthy motivator. Clingy relationships won't work for you. Being in a committed relationship gives you a strong sense self-confidence.

Juno in Taurus

There is a strong need for longevity in relationships with you. In a relationship you are looking for the comforts a relationship brings, a sense of "having" someone. You need an easy going partner who enjoys the comforts of home, food, and the nice things in life. A committed relationship brings you a sense of security. As a couple you may focus on the material things in life, a house, a nice car, etc.

Juno in Gemini

You will attract a mate that is very expressive, talkative and multi-faceted. Communication is key for any relationship, and in your case you can double that statement. You need to have daily communication and understanding to feel fulfilled. You need someone who enjoys a variety of activities and does not mind change. This sign placement can indicate more than one marriage. You will not do so well in clingy relationships, as you need one who trusts you enough not to question you when you are apart. A very busy schedule is indicated for your partner with this position. You must have trust as well.

Juno in Cancer

Commitment for you means someone who will nurture you and take care of you. Living together and starting a family is important to you. You also enjoy taking care of your partner. You need a strong emotional connection for yourself and your significant other to maintain the relationship. You have to see your marriage partner as the father or mother to your children.

Juno in Leo

Your partner will be very outgoing, strong willed, a little dramatic and will make you feel proud to be with them. You attract self-confident partners. You look for a partner who can have fun, see the town, go to concerts, the movies, and even travel the world in style and class. You need to feel dignified in your relationship. You also feel stronger and more confident in a relationship.

Juno in Virgo

Your partner will be analytical and very practical, a very good organizer and down to earth. You may be a bit meticulous in finding the right person to be with. Remember no one is perfect, rather we all are. Your relationship may involve you working together. You and your partner may be very health conscious, so that you both enjoy, eating right, going to the gym, living well. You are looking for a "clean", straight-laced partner. You need someone who can help organize you.

Juno in Libra

This is an excellent placement for Juno. Relationships are very important to you. You need fairness, and equality in your relationship. Your partner will be very sociable, cooperative and refined. You really want someone to share with, to be the other half. Art, music, and performing arts may appeal to you as a couple. Juno does not like being without a partner in Libra.

Juno in Scorpio

You seek a strong, magnetic and mysterious partner. You are looking for the "till death do us part", type of relationship. You need a relationship in which the two of you are completely emerged in passion. There is a strong sexual desire with Juno in Scorpio, sex is a must. Your partner will be a strong and silent type, but very deep and emotional .

Juno in Sagittarius

You need lots of freedom in your relationships. You don't like to be confined or pinned down, so when you do commit, it needs to be with someone who is not worried if you're not with them 24/7. You may need to have the same belief system in your relationship, like religion or philosophy of life. Many with this placement marry only into their own religion. You need a mate who is open minded, a free thinker, who is optimistic and adventurous.

Juno in Capricorn

Your partnership needs depend on structure, and security.

This may be the reason you marry. Your partner will be ambitious, a bit older, and very career minded. He or she will be climbing the ladder of success which is another item you look for in long term committed relationships. There is a sense of formality and tradition you seek in your relationship.

Juno in Aquarius

You need friendship in your relationship, which may seem strange to others, as you can be friends, with your partner. This is a sign of independence and uniqueness so you may not have the traditional relationships like others. There may be open relationships, polyamorous, or even if totally exclusive a sense of freedom and trust must be there. Through your relationship together you both find your individuality. You tend to encourage each other to be your unique selves.

Juno in Pisces

You are looking for the 'Soul Mate', the idealistic fantasy type of partner, Cinderella or Superman. The good news is that you will find one with this placement. Spirituality is highly important in your long term committed relationships. Romance is important, as well as lots of emotion. Your partner is very creative, spiritual, psychic and empathetic. You look to escape in your relationships from the everyday troubles life brings us.

JUNO IN THE HOUSES

Juno in the First House

You have very strong feelings and beliefs about marriage and commitment. Relationships are very important to you, and you may focus on this continuously until you're in one. You develop your own identity through being in a relationship. Your partner will help guide you or develop what you need to be more "yourself". You identify yourself as the other half.

Juno in the Second House

Marriage may be a symbol of monetary security for you, as it has for many others over the years. Marriage is also strongly valued in the second house. You may make money as a marriage officiant, wedding planner, or by selling women's goods.

Juno in the Third House

As they say "the key to any relationship is communication", especially a committed relationship. You may talk a lot about your relationship, your relationship needs or your partner. You may find your spouse through a sibling or neighbor. You communicate easily with your other half.

Juno in the Fourth House

You love your home life with your other half. You focus your relationship through your home life, and everything centers around family and domestic situations. Entertainment is often at your residence with your significant other being the host.

Juno in the Fifth House

You and your partner enjoy spending time on mutual hobbies, creative interests, or sports. You may enjoy entertaining or a night on the town, even speculation and gambling may be something you enjoy together. Of course children bring you together and are a major focus for you.

Juno in the Sixth House

You may work together with your significant other, or you have met at work. Health matters are important to the two of you, the gym, hiking, and physical fitness is important to you. Similar tastes in food, and hygiene your daily routine and habits are copacetic.

Juno in the Seventh House

Marriage or a committed relationship is highly important to you. You love having a significant other. Equality and fairness is very important. Your life is very intertwined with your partner more so than in most relationships. Relationships are vital to you.

Juno in the Eighth House

Your relationship is going bring be a huge transformation for you, catharsis happens due to your partnership. You love on a deep level, as in the 'til-death-do-us-part, type of relationship. Shared recourses are paramount, and finances are so intertwined you cannot tell what is who's after a while. Wills and legacies are important, your other half may receive a significant inheritance from their birth family.

Juno in the Ninth House

Your relationship may involve lots of long distance travel, and you may meet your spouse in another country. Intellectual pursuits are important for this relationship. Religion is a big deal for you and your mate, or at least your belief systems. You and your spouse like to spend time in the outdoors, having fun, enjoying sports.

Juno in the Tenth House

Your spouse may be heavily involved in a career, or perhaps you're both executive types. Marriage is a high ranking status symbol for tenth house Junos. Tradition is important and marriage is an honor for you. You may share a career with your partner. Your career may be Juno related; the marriage industry, or selling of merchandise related to marriage. Wedding planner, officiant, florist, wedding cakes etc

Juno in the Eleventh House

You will be friends with your significant other, you may have started out that way or been introduced by friends. You may enjoy being with friends as a couple. When someone mentions your name, they automatically think of your partner as well. The two of you spend much time in public, and with groups of people.

Juno in the Twelfth House

You had a past life relationship with your partner. This is a very karmic relationship in nature, truly you have been together many times. This relationship gets to the root of your subconscious behaviors, helping to heal or bring about change of issues and problems from the past. You have a psychic link with your spouse. Your partner may be psychic or work behind the scenes.

JUNO IN ASPECT

Juno Conjunction Sun

You are a very committed person in your personal relationships, and especially regarding marriage or committed relationships. You have strong beliefs about loyalty and are a devout and loyal person. You are dedicated to your family and the one you hold dear to your heart will always have a strong hold on you. You desire to be in a relationship with a person of strong power, and a big personality and ego. You may identify yourself through your partnerships which can lead to co-dependency if you don't keep your own boundaries clear. You like being in charge of things, you will be a ruler or co-ruler on some level. Your marriage will be a happy one, unless other factors show differently.

Juno Sextile Sun

You have a strong personality, one that likes to be in charge of things, and people. You will attract strong people into your life and will be sought after by many suitors desiring you for a marriage partner. You will have no problem being in a committed long term relationship, and you may have to choose which of the many will occupy your time. Once committed to someone, you may never change your mind. You believe strongly in vows, and commitments in relationships. Your marriage will be happy and easy going, and long lasting.

Juno Square Sun

There may be many challenges in your personal relationships, with ego presenting particular difficulty. You attract strong willed individuals and you are also strong willed, and you don't like being challenged or told what to do. You actually love your freedom and can have a difficult time committing to a relationship with one person. It's mostly that you just don't want to be controlled, or have to answer to a partner whom in the long run may cause problems for you. When are about thirty years old you may be more compromising than prior to the age of thirty. You want total commitment and may be a little jealous and revengeful if your other half is not completely loyal. Be sure to be clear on defining what commitment means between the two of you.

Juno Trine Sun

You will attract harmonious relationships, especially the significant one to which you commit yourself. You favor long term commitments and marriage, it will work out well for you and most likely at a pretty young age. You love commitment, and will enjoy being in one-on-one relationships. Your partner will be loyal as well, and you both will enjoy the same things in life as you are very compatible. Ceremonies and rituals will be important to you in life.

Juno Opposition Sun

Relationships may be very challenging and difficult for you. Commitment may be a foreign or bad word, as you like and enjoy your personal freedom, and marriage just may not seem like it is for you. You are capable of being married or in a committed long term relationship it will just take a little work, and you need to find someone who will allow you to be you, and not a very clingy, or needy type, as you won't work well with this type. If you go to battle with your partner this can be a very nasty situation, revenge, and score-keeping can be present. Try not to become the bickering couple so common in long term relationships.

Juno Conjunction Moon

You will feel especially comforted, and in an 'emotional good space' when in a committed relationship. There will be lots of emotional affection in your long term relationships, including marriage. You will attract one who will be the care-giving individual, and you yourself like taking care of others especially your other half. Marriage is important to you, to feel whole. Having a family will also be an important role for you. Marriage and commitment is very important for your emotional wellbeing.

Juno Sextile Moon

You will have a strong emotional bond with your marriage partner or long term relationship. There will be mutual feelings of wellbeing between the two of you. Communication and ideas flow very easily between you. There is a strong sense of commitment that makes you feel emotionally secure. Relationships between your partner and your mother should also go harmoniously.

Juno Square Moon

There may be emotional conflict between you and your other half, in marriage. Be sure to express what you need emotionally for yourself and ask directly what their needs are as well. There can be jealousy and if your ideas on commitment differ this could be very troublesome. Make sure you marry someone who has the same ideals in marriage and commitment as you do.

You may resist marriage altogether with a fear of commitment being the root cause. Your mother and your spouse may have a difficult time relating to one another.

Juno Trine Moon

Your relationships that are long term and committed, such as in marriage, will be very harmonious and easy going. Shared vision of what commitment is will coincide with you both. You have emotional compatibility with your partner making you feel emotionally secure in your relationship. Your mother and your other half will get along famously with each other and there is lots of family support for the two of you.

Juno Opposition Moon

You may have a hard time relating emotionally to your marriage partner. Your feelings about commitment and marriage may not match well with your partners own ideas. Be sure to talk about this in complete honesty with potential mates to avoid this conflict. Are you marriage material? Are they? What do you value, and what do you feel your needs to be in a relationship? This can be a very difficult relationship if you can't get along emotionally or your domestic lifestyles are so completely off.

Juno Conjunction Mercury

You communicate well with your other half, you talk to each other directly and this is the key to a happy and successful relationship. You may seem like friends which is a good thing in relationships. Sharing the same intellectual interests is also rewarding for your married life. Be sure to pick someone with whom you communicate easily, as it is very important for you to be able to speak openly with your partner.

Juno Sextile Mercury

Relationships should run very smoothly for you as you communicate well and on a regular basis with your partner. You stimulate each other's ideas and keep the conversation and the thought process exciting. This encourages each other to do their best and to feel free to be honest and open with each other. You would work well with each other on projects or even on the job together, as you could keep each other engaged and not become bored.

Juno Square Mercury

In your committed relationships and/or marriage, communication can be very difficult as you both have completely different ideas about how to talk to each other. There will be lots of disagreements with your partner and differing ideas, and your communication styles need to be addressed in order for your marriage to work. One of you may not talk much, or has a difficult time expressing when speaking with you. Work diligently on this so you can have better relationships on a personal level.

Juno Trine Mercury

Your communication with your spouse is very harmonious and positive. There is mutual understanding with your communication styles within the relationship. You find many interesting things to talk about, and it makes you a stronger couple. You may talk a lot about your spouse to others – in a good way of course. You both share many common interests. Decisions are made with involvement between you both.

Juno Opposition Mercury

There may be frequent arguments and misunderstandings with your domestic partner. Be sure to work daily on communication skills in the relationship, as this is a weak area in your chart which needs to be addressed to have better understanding between yourself and your partners. Arguing will take place if one assumes what the other is thinking. Don't make assumptions in your relationships any more than you would with your friends.

Juno Conjunction Venus

You will marry the one you love, you are very lucky in this respect. Venus the Goddess of love is conjunct Juno the Goddess of Marriage: Love and Marriage together. This is most fortunate. You will have mutual attraction and affection towards one another, and your relationship will be very harmonious and amicable. You find each other very attractive and have many of the same tastes in style, dress, music, and art. There is strong commitment given and expected in your relationships.

Juno Sextile Venus

You and your spouse or partner will get along famously and be mutually in love. This aspect shows much dedication, honesty and faithfulness in the relationship. You both share many of the same ideas and/or concepts. You and your partner share compatible tastes in music and the arts. Your marriage should be a very happy one.

Juno Square Venus

There can be an element of jealousy in your relationship with your spouse. It may be that you both have different values and especially in what commitment means in a relationship. Each person or couple has different commitment needs and desires, there is no right or wrong, it's just that both have to be in agreement on those issues. Make sure you both feel the same way about marriage before you enter into it. You both may have very different tastes in food, style, clothing or in the arts.

Juno Trine Venus

You get along exceptionally well with your spouse or other half, marriage should work out well for you as you attract a highly compatible person. You share many of the same tastes in music, the arts, style and clothing. Décor in the house will also be mutually appealing. This is a very harmonious aspect for long term committed relationships.

Juno Opposition Venus

Marriage may come late for you, if that is even something you're looking for. You need to decide what your commitment needs are in relationships, so you can find the correct partner that has the same needs. Relationships that are clingy or smothering will make you crazy, and cause you to run for the hills. You may be amenable to having an open or non-committal relationship. It may be that you are in a marriage or commitment but have very different backgrounds and therefore differing value systems. Sometimes this happens when people from different cultures marry or there are major age differences. Just be clear about what your needs are in a committed relationship, and follow through with your needs.

Juno Conjunction Mars

Your marriage may be a battle ground. This can be a long lasting marriage but the marriage is going to be hot and cold at times. Make sure you both have the same idea of what commitment is, if it is violated it will be war at best. This is a combination of the bickering couple who agrees on nothing. Strongly independent is what you both are, and both need that outlet. Retaliation and keeping a score card are common with this aspect. There may be a theme of competition in the relationship which can be healthy if it helps each one to strive to be the best that they can be. There can be much accomplished in this relationship if they work together in harmony. A great outlet would be working out at the gym together using the Mars energy in a positive way, maybe from different sides of the fence.

Juno Sextile Mars

You have an adventurous relationship with your partner. Activities that require physical energy are good for your relationship. This will help so that the Mars energy is used in healthy ways and doesn't turn into fighting. Hiking, going to the gym and a healthy sexual relationship are excellent activities with this placement. There can be competition in the relationship which can be very healthy if it keeps you both on the right track.

Juno Square Mars

Your marriage can be quite a challenge as you two are often completely at odds in many ways. This can be a highly stimulating relationship, which will require lots of compromise and team work in order to avoid quarrels. Your spouse may be irritable and the relationship can be very edgy and a constant struggle if you don't try to understand each other's individuality and needs. Much give and take is needed for this relationship to be healthy and survive over a period of time. You enjoy a strong partner who knows what they want – make sure you know what you want as well.

Juno Trine Mars

You and your spouse have a healthy competition and lots of spark when you are together, this works out harmoniously when you allow each other to do your own unique activities. Team work is indicated within your marriage, you seem to like the same activities and work well with each other on projects. This placement indicates a strong sexual attraction, that goes beyond just desire, interest in long term commitment is indicated. Exercise is a healthy outlet for you to do as a couple.

Juno Opposition Mars

Your marriage can be a battle ground, as you have total opposite ways of doing things. This can cause a lot of irritation with each other leading to fights. Positive ways for you to counter this is working on different projects separately so you don't get on each other's nerves and still can accomplish a lot. Make sure you have the same thoughts about what a committed relationship entails so there is no miscommunication with each other. Your spouse may be highly energetic and a go getter. You are attracted to a partner who is very self-assured and knows what they want.

Juno Conjunction Jupiter

This placement is an indication of a happy and healthy marriage. Your spouse may be very supportive of you, both emotionally and financially as well as overall good for you. Your partner will assist you in your growth which indicates a happy relationship. This is a good karmic placement for marriage. You may enjoy studying different philosophies and traveling abroad, you can even be from radically different cultures.

Juno Sextile Jupiter

Marriage is good for you, leading to growth and new opportunities that you may not have had otherwise, or prior to marriage. New philosophies and perspectives on life can come through your relationship. You feel a sense of ease with your other half. Your partner may lead you into new opportunities in career or life direction in general.

Juno Square Jupiter

You may have opposite view points in life philosophy, or religious views with your marriage partner. You may have come from completely different back grounds or socio–economic structures. Values and ideals will need to be put on the table so you both understand each other clearly. This can be a strong marriage it's just that you are from different worlds so to speak and there may be some compromise or adjusting going on to keep the peace.

Juno Trine Jupiter

You will have a great married life as this placement indicates. You attract a mate that is highly compatible with you and that is very good for your well being. You get along famously with each other. You may be good friends as well as lovers. Long distance travel may be a shared goal and reality for you. Your spouse may be highly educated.

Juno Opposition Jupiter

Although there is a lot of attraction between you and your partner, your marriage can be a somewhat difficult relationship coming from very different backgrounds or upbringing. Cultural differences may prevail in this case also. You can be at odds with your marriage partner as well, especially regarding commitment and what that exactly means to the both of you.

Juno Conjunction Saturn

You are likely to marry when you are a little older or after age thirty. You are also most likely to marry someone older than yourself. There may be a lot of responsibility to your partner, that can feel like obligation or duty. This does indicate a long term reliable relationship which is solid. Sometimes this can indicate a marriage to someone out of responsibility rather than strong attraction.

Juno Sextile Saturn

New opportunities that were not previously available to you prior to your marriage will present themselves once married. You will have a strong, long lasting marriage, most likely after the age of thirty. Your marriage indicates strong responsibility for each other and you help each other out with career goals. Your partner may bring those opportunities to you through your marriage.

Juno Square Saturn

With this placement your marriage will be delayed until after thirty, possibly even later in life. You may choose not to marry. Your may have to serve as care-giver to your partner, whether incapacitated or some other debility, you will be the one "parenting" or responsible for your partner. This does not mean an unhappy marriage. You are likely to have this feeling that you must take care of your spouse, no matter what, as if it is karmic in nature.

Juno Trine Saturn

Marriage takes you to higher stations in life, more than you imagined. There may be a certain prestige that the marriage brings. Maybe the spouse is well to do, or an accomplished executive in the chosen field. Regardless, this is a strong marriage. You may marry someone older or with status above your own, such as a boss. You enjoy the security and the structure of a reliable and structured relationship. Mutual responsibilities of taking care of each other are indicated with this aspect.

Juno Opposition Saturn

Marriage may seem restrictive to you, as you need to be your own individual, and you certainly won't want to marry until you have your own "career" or life calling started and well under way. You are not going to have someone throw you off your course, so that fear is what keeps you from getting too close, or marrying at a young age. You take marriage very seriously and eventually, later in life you will most likely marry someone older. Once in a committed relationship you will honor and cherish it, as you will love the security it brings.

Juno Conjunction Uranus

You have very different views of marriage. They may not be traditional and they don't have to be. Relationship rules or agreements should be up to the two involved and no one else's opinion should matter. You will have unique people who are very individualistic enter your life in the relationship area. You need to keep your individuality and that is what keeps you from traditional relationships. Open marriage may appeal to you and be totally acceptable as long as it is with your partner as well. This placement says you will attract very unusual people from very different backgrounds than your own, keeping your relationships very exciting. Don't try to fit in the same box as everyone else, that isn't you.

Juno Sextile Uranus

You will have unusual partnerships especially in committed relationships. You attract progressive, and innovative individuals into your life. You enjoy the excitement in the instability of change, as many relationships are indicated in your life. Your marriage will be on your own terms. Keeping your individuality is highly important to you and to your partner as well. Whatever the case it works for you. You may start out as friends, long before you commit to your partner.

Juno Square Uranus

The thought of being in a committed relationship with one person scares you. You don't want to be restricted or feel restrained in a relationship. You've got to be you. This is indicative more than one marriage if you marry too young or someone who tries to restrict you. You are able to be in a happy and committed relationship its just that you need to find someone who will let you be you, and not too clingy or jealous. Make your own terms for commitment and you will be happy. This is one of the planetary placements that is okay with "open relationships".

Juno Trine Uranus

Your marriage is sure to be exciting and not a run of the mill type. You enjoy the thrill and excitement of being in a relationship. You attract a partner who brings out the uniqueness of you, as you both love adventure and trying new and unusual events. People may not understand your relationship and they don't need to. It's the business of you and your partner, and no one else. Don't worry about conventionality, that isn't you. Many relationships are fulfilling whether they get a legal document or not. Your other half will be as unique and different as they come, which is why you are with each other.

Juno Opposition Uranus

Relationships are certainly not what everyone else's looks

like. This may bother you as you would like a traditional marriage, or maybe it's your other half that this is making crazy. The two of you may be strongly attracted, but don't agree on what a committed relationship is. One wants a traditional marriage the other wants to have just a committed relationship or even an open relationship. You can work it out. Just give each other the ability and the freedom to be who they really are, no restrictions.

Juno Conjunction Neptune

You are very dreamy and idealistic about your marriage partner and marriage itself. Marriage may seem like a fairy tale to you. You need to be careful not to put your partner on a pedestal as a Super Man or Wonder Woman remember everyone has flaws and no one is perfect. You may attract a partner who has addiction or alcohol issues and you just need to be aware of what co-dependency is and what it means, so you don't become the co-dependent spouse that has no identity of their own. On another level you may be looking for a spouse who is very spiritual and a "soul" mate. You may very well attract the soul mate you are looking for with this aspect.

Juno Sextile Neptune

Your partner will be very romantic, and dreamy in nature, with a strong sense of spirituality. Marriage will be very romantic for you, as you and your spouse seem to tune in to each other almost psychically. You enjoy music and the arts together, and this is an ideal marriage. Your spouse inspires you in your creativity and spirituality.

Juno Square Neptune

Relationships may seem confusing to you, especially in committed relationships. Before you actually get married make sure you both know each other inside and out so you don't get mislead or deceived by outward appearances and secret pasts. You may marry someone who is needy in some way either mentally or physically. You and your partner may have differing beliefs about spirituality and religion. This aspect cautions against alcohol and drugs being misused by a partner.

Juno Trine Neptune

You may feel a sense of ecstasy with your marriage partner as if they were your divine partner. This aspect favors a relationship where both enjoy and inspire each other on a deeper level, a "soul" level. There is a strong psychic connection between you and your other half. You both enjoy the same sense of art and music with each other. This is a harmonious marriage based on strong trust and love, that goes beyond the physical.

Juno Opposition Neptune

Marriage may be disappointing for you if you don't learn who to trust and who not to. You have grand ideals about marriage which may not be realistic, but more fantasy driven which leads to disappointment. You can find your soul mate once you first discover your own true self, before looking to find happiness in another. You may have to take care of a needy person or someone who is self-medicating.

Juno Conjunction Pluto

You attract rather intense relationship partners, who tend to try to control you. Be careful of manipulative power plays in your committed relationships, trying to control one another is not fun for either party and doesn't give much happiness in the marriage. Marriage will certainly be transformative for you, as you learn how to truly share with another individual on this planet. Your marriage will be very deep, giving you lots of soul growth. This aspect indicates that you don't think a relationship or marriage should end until "death do us part".

Juno Sextile Pluto

Your marriage will be very intense and will bring you to

many transformations, that further benefit you in the big picture of your life. You certainly do attract those who are passionate about everything they do. You enjoy the deepness of the relationship, sharing with your marriage partner will not be like any of the others, before that were non-committal. Many new opportunities arise due to this relationship for you.

Juno Square Pluto

You have many power plays going on in your relationship, that go very deep. This intensity may be too much for you to deal with. This aspect does indicate a divorce or separation of at least one major relationship. You will be a different person due to your committed relationships and the effect they have on you. Be careful not to invoke jealousy in this relationship. Your marriage partner will be very passionate, intense and deep.

Juno Trine Pluto

You attract powerful people with whom you can have committed relationships. This ultimately benefits you in the long run of your life. Your spouse is a very powerful and influential person in your life together. You both have intense marital desires within that help empower one another. Marriage has a powerful, positive effect on your life.

Juno Opposition Pluto

Your marriage may be very intense and at times turbulent and powerfully transformative. You and your partner should not try to control each other and no tit for tat games either. Revenge and manipulation should also be avoided; if this is present you may want to consider that your relationship is toxic, or that this situation may be very much needed for your growth. This aspect does show a relationship that is very powerful and intriguing. Try not to force change upon one another, and instead help each other with your personal goals, if you do this nothing can stop this relationship.

Juno Conjunction Pallas

Your marriage partner will be strong, independent, and very much a strategist and planner. There will be a strong need for approval from your mate to make you feel connected. Politics, work, and career are good topics of like interests that you both share. Creativity is honored and shared between the two of you. Your partner may be a lawyer, or at least very career oriented.

Juno Sextile Pallas

Your partner may be very busy and extremely career oriented. You look for someone who is very good at organizing and planning events for the two of you. It may be best if your partner is in charge of the finances for the relationship. You need a relationship where you share creativity and intellectual pursuits together.

Juno Square Pallas

You may have conflicts or disagreements over philosophies, concepts, creative ideas or ideals. You may have a completely different background intellectually with your partner which can be a challenge for the both of you to communicate or stimulate each other intellectually. Artistic style and creative pursuits may be another area of disagreement. These can be worked on and in some cases easily dealt with, it's just a matter of honoring the differences with in the relationship and what you learn from each other.

Juno Trine Pallas

You will have many of the same or similar tastes with your partner in the creative and academic realms. You and your other half are supportive and encouraging to each other with your inventive, creative, and scholastic pursuits, assisting in your overall compatibility in the relationship.

Juno Opposition Pallas

In your committed relationships there will likely be challenges around intellectual, scholastic, and creative endeavors. You both simply have different or opposite tastes. This is why there is an attraction. To balance out these differences, embrace them. It may be difficult to talk with each other unless you meet in the middle to find common ground, rather than agreeing to disagree.

Juno Conjunction ASC

Juno on your ascendant gives you some of the traits of Juno whether male or female. You view marriage as a onetime deal, no plans to divorce, it must be totally committed. And vows of marriage are extremely important to you. You look at marriage as a contract, and it is something you desire to be totally involved and enmeshed with another individual. There can be the negatives also, such as, jealousy, tit for tat, score-keeping and revengefulness when slighted or wronged.

Juno Sextile ASC

You see marriage as an opportunity and something you look forward to. You will be one hundred percent committed to your partner, a vow is a vow. You may think of marriage quite a bit, or of your marriage (partner) often.

Juno Square ASC

The thought of commitment or marriage to someone may give you an uncomfortable feeling. You may have seen the challenges your parents had while you were growing up and related that to how a marriage is, or is supposed to be. Frightening to some, and to others a beautiful thing, regardless it is a challenge to live and commit to anyone. That is your challenge: to find someone who can relate and get along with you. Just be yourself, don't try to be anyone else, or please just to please, in the long run you will find the correct person for you.

Juno Trine ASC

You will enjoy lots of creative fun with your partner. Travel, leisure and amusement will be key in your relationship. Children will play an important role in the marriage with this aspect. You will find a harmonious and committed partner to be with. You believe in the sanctity of marriage.

Juno Opposition ASC

Your partner will be very committed to you and that is what you feel a marriage should be. Power and control can be an issue with this placement. Be sure to balance to power and control in the relationship to keep it equal. That is what your partner wants. If it is not given, there is a strong likelihood of a power play or manipulation games.

Juno Conjunction MC

You may find your marriage partner through your career or you may work with your partner. Your other half will be career minded as well. You see your marriage as an important position or status in society. Marriage may even be equal to your career goal(s) – it may even be the goal. You may work in an industry involving weddings, catering, and wedding planning, such as a wedding officiant. You may be the second in command or vice president of a company as Juno is second in power to Zeus.

Juno Sextile MC

This is an excellent placement for career. You will have good partnership(s) in the career arena. This means with bosses, or literal business partners. Your marriage partner will support your career and will be accommodating to your success.

Juno Square MC

There may be some challenges with your significant other and your career. It may be that you spend so much time working that you have to create quality time with your spouse, and family.

Juno Trine MC

This placement shows your commitment to your career is strong, and that there is a role of power in your chosen field. You may be a supervisor, manager or boss of some kind. In your personal relationships this aspect shows a strong supportive spouse with regard to your career, who will be there for you.

Juno Opposition MC

This aspect is a difficult one due to the desire for a career and a happy home life with your family. Time is the challenge here, spending enough time at home and away from work is the main issue. Work to insure there is quality time with your partner.

Juno conjunction Chiron

Marriage may be what you have longed for all your life. Your partner may be the one to assist you in your healing, and be a mentor, teacher and coach for you. You may marry a healer or a doctor.

Juno Sextile Chiron

You may be a protector of the powerless, and a crusader for their rights. Children, animals, and even the earth are of interest to you in protecting the underdogs. Your partner may be a healer, doctor or involved in teaching in some way.

Juno Square Chiron

There may be issues and concerns about commitment in your relationships. Did your parents have these issues? Do you have trust issues regarding fidelity? The challenge is to learn to trust again in order to have a great working relationship in your marriage.

Juno Trine Chiron

Relationships are very healing and powerful for you. Your mate may be a true mentor, and teacher to you and very therapeutic for you to be with. The trust is strong between the two of you. Relationships in general are very good.

Juno Opposition Chiron

In order to have healthy committed relationships, you will first need to address your own healing issues. This will enable your relationships to go so much smoother and happier, than if you attempt to project healing responsibilities onto your partner. There may be issues over past relationships that did not honor the vows of the relationship. This can prevent you from going forward in partnerships until resolved. Start to trust again.

PALLAS ATHENA

GODDESS OF WISDOM

Goddess of wisdom, higher mind, the intellect coupled with intuition, seeing both sides of the picture.

Key Words/Themes:

Strategy; she was a strategist coming up with the battle plans etc., resolving issues without conflict if possible. Resolutions. Inventor, trainer, politician, law and justice, equality and fairness. Psychic, mind-healing, hypnosis, creative visualization, manifesting. Battle plans, plan of attack. Being able to see the big picture through small details.

Totem: Owl representing wisdom.

City: Athens named for her.

Other name: Minerva, Athena

PALLAS IN THE SIGNS

Pallas in Aries

Your perception is highly instinctual and primitive. You see quickly and naturally the "battle plan", or "plan of attack" In any given situation. You operate keenly, rapidly, and forcefully if needed. Your intuition is spontaneous, needing immediate action in many cases. You see clearly how to start and initiate projects, how to get things rolling. You're the champion at quick witted challenges. You would do well in a career where you can execute this ability, a strategic planner, project engineer for example.

Pallas in Taurus

You are very creative in the material realms, with a talent for knowing the value of things, especially great at financial planning and a budgeting wizard. You are great at making things, from manufacturing to knitting sweaters you are highly perceptive in how to make things. With a natural talent for money planning you know how to earn money and make a living even with just the basics. You would do well in the healing arts such as massage therapy, or hands on healing. Your artistic side is strong.

Pallas in Gemini

You have a highly perceptive mind, quite active especially in communications, you're a "word-smith". You can often see clearly how to do things in duality, that is in two different scenarios at the same time, evaluating which one will work best. Working with affirmations is especially good for you, to manifest what you visualize by saying the spoken word you will quickly create what you desire. You are very observant of body language when talking and relating to people. You have clever and sharp insights into people and situations. This is a great placement for singers, lyricists, and writers.

Pallas in Cancer

You are highly perceptive and intuitive into what people are feeling, you're a natural empath, with very accurate psychic impressions. You have the ability to see clearly into family matters and dynamics. This placement shows that you also know how to nurture people, you naturally know what they need for comfort. Entertaining can be celebrated in the home with family, and being a cook or chef is a natural for you. Trust in your gut level impressions as they are your body's way of first letting you know your psychic ability is on track, it will be correct.

Pallas in Leo

This placement is highly creative whether it be in the arts, starting your own business or some kind of performance, you possess huge potential in these areas. You are a great leader as you see how to lead and motivate others to do what you need done, you would make a great boss. You are best in leadership, being the boss or being self-employed, it may be to hard to be the employee. You know how to create. Creative visualization is a good practice for you to explore, as you are a natural at it. You may have to show strength and bravery in your work. This placement favors, the performing arts, music and acting.

Pallas in Virgo

Your motto may be DIRFT: Do it right the first time. You are a perfectionist, and are very perceptive in analyzing systems, procedures and getting tasks done. You see the big picture starting with the small details first. You're a detailed strategist, leaving nothing undone or unchecked. You can see how to get the job done, great placement for supervising or teaching. You are great at tasks with many minute details that need attention. Crafts like sewing, woodworking, or even mechanics is favored with this placement.

Pallas in Libra

This placement gives a strong sense of justice, and interest in fairness and equality. There may also be interest in judicial systems, and politics. You have very keen insights into relationships and the dynamics of couples. You are a great counselor and may even find work in this area. This placement favors decorators, designers, and lawyers, as well as relationship counselors or human resources managers.

Pallas in Scorpio

You leave nothing uncovered when you are interested in something. You use your logic and analyze the small details, and use your intuition for the missing pieces giving you the big picture. This gives you a strong psychic ability, especially to see what motivates others, and the psychology involved. You get to the bottom line of the situation. Pallas in Scorpio is interested in detective work, psychic realms, hypnosis, mind over matter, and can be very skilled in these areas. Healing with the mind is very natural to you.

Pallas in Sagittarius

You have the ability to see the big picture in the scheme of things. Broad vision, and expanded interests in many subjects keeps you always searching for the truth and higher knowledge. You have a love of higher education, whether it be in life or in an actual classroom. You do learn from experience and through others, especially other cultures to which you're drawn. You possess strong humor, to keep perspective, and balance. You are seeking the truth, this may involve your religious belief system, or philosophy of life.

Pallas in Capricorn

Seeing how to manage an organization, situation or structure is a strong ability you possess. This gives you executive ability in management, and in the process of your own life. Using creative visualization you will manifest your desires, and visions very quickly as Capricorn is an Earth element sign, in the Cardinal family. This means you are great at seeing things through to fruition, and you have the discipline needed to get it there. Trust your intuition in business and you won't go wrong. You would be good in the business, stock-market, and financial arenas.

Pallas in Aquarius

You perceive your objectives and goals in a very progressive way. You are very inventive, and creative in new ways of doing things that interest you, as the old is boring and outdated. You have a genius mind that can perceive how things can be. You see the future ideal of how things could be, and then the ability to get it there. You have a way of suddenly knowing things without rational thinking, it's the way your intuition works; you're just "downloaded" in an instant with the information needed, and then you just "know".

Pallas in Pisces

Your perception is highly psychic, and creative. You have a dreamy and mystical side to you, as your imagination is very strong and active. You may dismiss things as coincidence or synchronicity, but you really are aware on another level. You learn and perceive through osmosis; learning by absorbing everything around you, which is so hard to tell where things begin and end. You are very interested in spirituality, spirit guides past lives etc… and you do have insight into them. Music, acting, poetry are all good expressions for you to follow.

PALLAS IN THE HOUSES

Pallas in the First house

You have a strategist type personality, a planner, very wise and broad minded. People come to you for counsel, and advice. Your intuition is high with this placement, and creative potential can border on genius. You possess a powerful personality. Your appearance may be somewhat androgynous with a first house placement.

Pallas in the Second house

You are excellent with planning your budget, (unless afflicted) and making the most of your spending money. You also are good at seeing how to make money, you have talent in giving advice about money, you would make an excellent financial planner.

Pallas in the Third house

You communicate very clearly and on purpose, no minced

words with you. Communication is strategic for you. This placement is excellent for writers. Your words, spoken or written, may seem planned or calculated. Your sibling (s) may be very Athena-like, focused, ambitious, intellectual. If you have a sister relations should be good between you. Good for writers, teachers, sales people.

Pallas in the Fourth house

You may analyze your family and the family dynamics with Pallas here. This may be due to trying to measure up to one of your parents. Your home will have lots of crafty items as Pallas rules over crafts. This placement is great for realtors, and multi-housing owners or developers. This is one of the intuitive houses so your intuition can be high with this placement, and psychic phenomena may run in the family.

Pallas in the Fifth house

Your creativity is high with many interests and hobbies, and maybe even inventions. This placement does lower the romantic side of this house as Pallas is more interested in utilizing the sexual energy for creating with art, music, inventions etc. You may be interested in Pallas archetypes for relationships or dating; androgynous, virginal, highly creative and intellectual.

Pallas in the Sixth house

You are very good at organizing, and making systems work. You would do well with a job that is highly analytical and technical. You're a natural healer with Pallas here, and may work in the health care industry, or with nutrition and food. This placement also is great for accountants and investigators. Any job that requires lots of detail and focus would be good for you. Pets and animals respond to you well, as you can communicate with them on another level.

Pallas in the Seventh house

Pallas in the seventh can describe your other half, who may be a strong planner and organizer, with very strong intuition, a psychic etc. You receive good advice and counsel from others often just in casual conversation. You have insight into relationships and how they work; this is a great placement for a relationship counselor, a lawyer or a politician.

Pallas in the Eighth house

You have amazing insight into the secrets of life; death, the occult, sexuality, and even joint finances. This is one of the psychic placements especially in mediumship – talking with the other side. This is great for careers as a tax accountant, financial planner, mortician, surgeon, sex industry, and psychology.

Pallas in the Ninth house

You have many keen insights into the philosophy of life, and love to study and learn from other cultures. You would do well as a politician, lawyer or judge with this placement. Metaphysical subjects may interest you as well – reincarnation, astrology, and ritual magic to name a few. Teaching higher knowledge is a skill you possess.

Pallas in the Tenth house

Career is where you shine, and a strong passion with Pallas in this house. The thrill of conquering your quest, planning and following through on your strategy keeps you enthralled in your chosen career. This placement is indicative of a Pallas type career; healing arts, psychic arts, inventor, law and justice, leader, manager or politician.

Pallas in the Eleventh house

In the area of hopes, wishes and dreams, Pallas gives you the ability to plan and determination to see things come to fruition. You tend to join in groups or clubs related to hobbies, crafts, music, and intellectual groups. Your friends may be very intellectual and intuitive sharing their perceptions and strategies with you. You are very good at seeing the big picture in group dynamics, making you a great team leader, and assigning people to the correct task. Excellent position for a human resource manager.

Pallas in the Twelfth house

You have a very strong and active subconscious mind. Pallas here gives you psychic insight into people and situations. You may remember past lives vividly. This placement gives interest into all things paranormal, psychics, mediums, Tarot cards, crystal balls, and spirits. Guidance is often asked of you just as it was for Pallas, you will be sought after for advice. You may be reluctant at first to show this side of yourself, preferring to stay behind the scenes. Other jobs include trouble-shooters from call centers, data processors, computer techs, and detectives, psychology, counselor.

PALLAS IN ASPECT

Pallas Conjunction Sun

You are an extremely creative individual in many areas. You understand the laws of manifestation and creation, so working with the law of attraction is natural for you. What this means is that you can manifest by visualizing with your mind's eye what you want to create, and with your strong intention and positive outlook things simply manifest for you. You may have interest in one of the following fields; justice, the arts, music, crafts, as well as judicial, and politics. You are a strategist as you see clearly the long-range outcome of things to come based on your assessment of the now.

Pallas Sextile Sun

You have many talents and opportunities for success with this placement in your chart. You have a very intuitive edge as you perceive the big picture even with little details of the present. Those little clues add up to big intuition and visions of the future. You are a natural analyst and strategist. You have a great deal of creative intelligence, and you can manifest whatever your heart desires with strong conviction and commitment.

Pallas Square Sun

You have a lot of creative potential in your life you just need to learn how to get out of your own way, to allow things to happen. You may be trying too hard or have doubts about whether you can succeed or not, which will cause situations to go south, resulting in manifesting not what you want – but what you did **not** want. The secret for you is to trust your intuition, and your creative and natural knowing side, and not get caught up in ego and pride or trying too hard, just allow things to take shape and they will. You may have been told you have to work hard – or that you work too hard at pleasing others especially your father, which is keeping you from your true talents.

Pallas Trine Sun

You have natural talents in many areas, such as healing, giving advice, and a plan of attack for those seeking your direction. You are a natural detective and can see the small details and the big picture that follows, and how things will turn out. You can succeed in many areas such as the arts, and music, judicial systems of law and justice, political arenas, and even in some cases if the chart agrees intuitive psychic arts like tarot cards, or other forms of divination.

Pallas Opposition Sun

You have a very ambitious nature and wanting to succeed is paramount to you. You may fear success and can at times sabotage the fruition of your dreams by getting in your own way. There may be conflicts with others about your plan of attack or strategy, this may take some integration time, and be sure there are not ego conflicts with others while planning a task. You have a strong sense of competition with others and like the challenge of winning a situation. Mental competition is what you are good at, figuring out the strategy of how to take down the opponent.

Pallas Conjunction Moon

You have a highly intuitive mind bordering heavily on the psychic side. Your feelings about things are spot on, as your intuitive Moon, which feels things, is working in tandem with intuitive Pallas and together they see the big picture. Pallas helps separate the strong emotion of the Moon making it more rational and logical. Pallas conjunction the Moon shows a very protective concern for children, and small animals.

Pallas Sextile Moon

This aspect gives you a smart and intellectual sense. You enjoy both sides of your nature, your soft and emotional side as well as your intellectual knowing side, as they are integrated well. With this aspect you can be a highly creative person in the arts, crafts or in the psychic arts, such as tarot, palmistry etc. Your intuition level is high and strong. Your memory should be very strong.

Pallas Square Moon

You need to learn to trust yourself, your psychic and natural knowing versus logic – integration of both is what is needed, and trust in yourself is the key. You may have issues trying to please everyone, especially your father which then can alienate your mother in a triangulation. You may have a hard time expressing your feelings as Pallas is not emotionally based, but more logical and detached, where your Moon is more sensitive and feeling.

Pallas Trine Moon

This aspect brings out the best of your intellect, and logical side with your feeling and instinctual side. You are natural detective and can read people very quickly and succinctly. You are a manifestor – someone who can manifest through the act of creative visualization. What you visualize and focus on with good feelings becomes reality, seemingly like magic. Use this talent and skill to improve your life and others.

Pallas Opposition Moon

There may have been conflicts with your early upbringing as you may have been taught not to show your feelings or you'll be seen as vulnerable. Intellectual parenting is great but it can be an issue when you don't get recognition unless you do well. There can also be conflicts with too much work on your plate to pay attention to your emotional and family needs. Your problem solving, logical side is in conflict with your emotions and feelings, try to integrate and resolve any emotional issues, especially if you're hearing "how my mother would think", then you know you're reacting to past conditioning.

Pallas Conjunction Mercury

You are a very intellectual thinker and strategist, always one step ahead of the game, with alternate plans of escape or rerouting. You have a political way of communicating in which you always seem to say the appropriate thing. Politically correct is okay as long as it doesn't take over and become people pleasing for the sake of argument – express your true thoughts. You may have interests in politics, strategic planning, architecture, mathematics, and the arts and crafts.

Pallas Sextile Mercury

You have a way of communicating that brings people together in thought, or in synch with each other. You are very politically correct and your thoughts are well planned before putting them into words. Writing would be a great subject for you, as you would be a great wordsmith. You love problem solving and coming up with solutions, this can be good for computer programmers and engineers.

Pallas Square Mercury

There can be difficulty in expressing your thoughts and words the way you intended. It is not a speech impediment, its just that you are so much in your head, and afraid of saying the wrong thing or even offending someone, so you try too hard. Planning a strategy and or making long term plans can be very hard for you, as you have difficulty seeing ahead and committing to a plan. There may be too many things that change, then what? With no plan you feel inadequate. Work on seeing plan A with plan B already in range if plan A fails, this way you won't' feel so insecure.

Pallas Trine Mercury

Your communication and writing skills are off the charts, you need to utilize this talent in some way. You have great foresight and therefore great skills in scheduling, planning and managing as your mind is always strategizing and ready for the next move. Problem solving is something you enjoy, and giving advice is something people will come to you for. This is a great position to have for a variety of jobs such as, managerial, human resources, writing, teaching, and the arts and crafts, not to mention politics. You also have a strong sense of intuition that doesn't let you down.

Pallas Opposition Mercury

Relationships can be difficult, especially over miscommunications and plans that don't manifest. Plans that change can really get to you, and it may seem to happen in relationships most often. Be more flexible when your plan of attack gets thwarted by another who changes everything last minute. Be sure to communicate and articulate what those plans are. Trusting your intuition is important here, and something you will need to learn to integrate into your life.

Pallas Conjunction Venus

You have a very creative and artistic side which can be used in many ways; making things look better, prettier, whether it is wood crafting, being a seamstress, or a salesmen of quality goods, there is talent here. You know how to make others feel good on the inside outside. You're skillful in using the right words to sway people to your side, using honey rather than other methods is your tactic. This is a good aspect for match making in love.

Pallas Sextile Venus

You have a very creative side, which can manifest in interest in music, the arts, and crafts, seamstress, or some other creative skill. You have a strong sense of charm and know just when to turn it on, and how to create harmony in your dealings. This aspect shows you know how to handle others and get along with them.

Pallas Square Venus

You may feel as if there is a blockage in your creative self potential. You may feel too intellectual and not artistic enough, or the creative side is there with no thoughts about how to execute this into manifestation. The challenge is to integrate your planning and execution side with the creative and artistic side.

Pallas Trine Venus

You may have many talents in the arts, music, decorating, or even landscape design, so how are you utilizing your creative energy? You have a good sense of follow through and of what it will take to complete a project. You have a way of making people feel harmonious as you know what to say or do, with your congenial personality.

Pallas Opposition Venus

It may be hard for you to put down your analytical and strategic mind for a moment to enjoy the luxuries and comforts of life. This can lead to issues in relationships especially with significant others. Integrate and balance work time with pleasure time, there is no need to feel guilty about indulging once in a while.

Pallas Conjunction Mars

You have a very strong will, and are great at the "plan of attack" in any situation especially where your self-defense needs come into play. This is a great aspect for working for the military in other areas of life, as it is good for getting the job done in the most efficient way. People will come to you and ask how to complete the project, making you a natural leader and managerial candidate. Strategy that uses logic may be the best way to fight the battle.

Pallas Sextile Mars

You have many talents. Your physical skills along with your incredible skills of perception would be excellent in sports that involve mental capacity with endurance. Karate is one sport from which you could benefit, but many others would also be good for you, even dance and aerobics. You have to get this energy out in a positive way. Throwing yourself into a project that requires both mental and physical skills are best for you. You would be a great marksman, target practice is calling you.

With your highly competitive spirit you love strategizing your plan of attack. This translates well into sports, as well as into your daily life but can even go into more of a career. Some organizations have strategic planners, military and/or political. You would be very good at debate and in the law arena, such as lawyer. You will be very active and you could also be a personal trainer. Other areas of interest may include hunting, gaming, and the medical field especially around surgery or quick response team, like in the emergency room.

Pallas Square Mars

Sometimes patience is what is best. This is hard for you as you can see what needs to be done and how, part of you just wants to jump ahead and do without the proper plan of attack. It will behoove you to heed this and practice utilizing the strategic planning as part of your routine: thought before action. You may have to smooth things over when you act without thinking first. This is an aspect that will get better as you mature and age, or learn quickly from your past mistakes.

Pallas Trine Mars

This placement is excellent for many specialized skills and training. Military is favored with this placement, and would be a great environment for the best use of this energy. Utilizing your perceptive and strategic skills with your physical endurance makes a great military person. Personal trainer, or life coach, dietary coaching, career planning specialist are all good uses of this energy. A surgeon would benefit with this placement.

Pallas Opposition Mars

You have a determined personality that can get in its own way – overzealous! You are extremely independent and willful. This has its good sides such as being able to work long, hard hours. This opposition is a battle of wits that you get yourself into with others over who is doing what, and how it is being done. You don't like to be told how to do something, you are better off working by yourself or in charge of others. This placement is not good for subordination.

Pallas Conjunction Jupiter

You have great social skills, using charm, and humor to get the point across is a real skill. This placement is great for teaching, mentoring and coaching on many different levels. You could even be a professor or scholar in a specialized field. You have a broad range of specialized knowledge. Career as a lawyer or politician would be good for you. You have a good relationship with your father or father figure, however you are always seeking his approval, learn to be your own support, and approve of yourself.

Pallas Sextile Jupiter

You have a keen intellect and strive to learn all you can. You have good political and social awareness and are good at seeing these topics in a progressive way. It's like you can see what is ahead for mankind in many ways, social, economic, and inventions yet to be discovered or invented, perhaps by you. You are fond of higher education and mind expansion, leaping ahead into the future. You have a great relationship with your father, getting along and being able to express your ideas with him. His approval is great for you and something you long for.

Pallas Square Jupiter

You may have issues with approval from your father, as you don't see eye to eye with his values and maybe even differing religious or spiritual views. You may not agree with the social norms and customs, as you see a different and more progressive way of thinking. Approval from father or the mainstream may not agree with your career choice, as it may be too out there for current thought. This aspect can produce pessimistic thinking and negative outlook if no encouragement comes from others.

Pallas Trine Jupiter

You have excellent talents for teaching, training and coaching others. As a mentor you give positive advice and acknowledgment. You see the big picture strategy for improving social systems or how to teach others to expand on what you taught them. You help others keep an open mind and to explore the possibilities that even you haven't yet thought of. An uncle may be a positive influence on your life.

Pallas Opposition Jupiter

You have to watch out for superiority complexes as you may have had pessimistic outlook on others that can make you feel a more inflated sense of self-importance. Disapproving of others can be a lack of self-confidence, as you are really seeking the approval of others. This may have been instilled in you as you did not get the positive response from elders that you were seeking. Many disagreements in viewpoint or opinion are indicated. Positive thinking and encouragement of others will change your life dramatically for the better, as you can be a master of the "Law of attraction".

Pallas Conjunction Saturn

You possess a great skill in concentration and focusing your attention to the details that make your projects successful. You are extremely disciplined with yourself at attaining your goals and dreams, as you work very diligently to attain them. You have great skill for project management, risk management, and managerial work as you see the big picture in the larger context. You are a very timely and hardworking individual with great focus and vision.

Pallas Sextile Saturn

You have a reputation for excellence that can't be denied as you are very talented in organizing and putting your vision into reality. Your talents include risk management, asset management, corporate vision and management of others. You had positive reinforcement from authority figures as you were growing up they gave you a great example to follow as well.

Pallas Square Saturn

This is a challenging aspect you have within you. Challenges may be difficult as you see the big picture and how things should be or could be. The challenge is the current structure or society's rules are not in agreement with your vision. This can create frustration and an attitude of giving up, if you're constantly told no. Getting looked over at promotion time is a result of this, you will have to work extra hard to get your view and vision heard and seen into fruition. Don't let this discourage you as it is meant to help you see that you are just ahead of your time and you will get there. Don't give up, you will succeed in the long run, it just won't be as easy as others have it. Limitations that lead to strength.

Pallas Trine Saturn

You have a great sense of timing in your ideas and the visions that you create. You seem to be able to manifest your ideas and dreams with relative ease compared to others. You make a great manager as you can see what needs to be done and the order and strategy that needs to happen to get it done. This is a huge skill and talent that you have over many others. Push your inventions and sudden ideas to the limit and you will manifest them in reality. Skills include corporate management, risk management, and you make a great project manager.

Pallas Opposition Saturn

You have had to learn through many disappointing career moves and transfers, the key is that you understand and learn what it wrong. How did you learn to correct the mistakes of the past? Some of these situations may seem like you had no choice and you may not have had a role in choosing these are life lessons from karma-bearer, Saturn. Learn discipline and focus and don't give up on your great visionary sense of the future, you will eventually manifest the success you have been seeking since childhood. You may have had an absence of parental training and discipline while you were growing up.

Pallas Conjunction Uranus

You have a very progressive vision and are an expert at manifesting your desires. Things seem to happen quickly and suddenly as you get ideas out of nowhere, and you feel compelled to act on them. That's your intuition talking: listen. You have a genius mind that is very quick and highly intelligent. You would excel at computer programing and computer skills in general. Astrology would be an excellent outlet for you to undertake as you would quickly grasp all the different symbols almost intuitively as if you have known them all along. Other great fields for you are science, technology, electricity, and any form of invention and ingenuity will suit you well.

Pallas Sextile Uranus

You have a very intellectual mind, that is very quick, and can see the outcome of many situations. You are an excellent strategic planner, and would work well in many inventive platforms, especially those that include technology, and computers. You have a strong sense of intuition that is so fast its like a lightning bolt strikes and then you know something.

Pallas Square Uranus

You are a rather unconventional person, who wants social change, and you are the person to make it happen. You can see how things "ought to be" and you rebel at the current state of affairs. Others may see you as erratic, and a rebel or a maverick. This can be good, if used in the correct way, be the one to positively create social change, think of new strategies to incorporate your ideals.

Pallas Trine Uranus

With your quick mind and strong intuition, you are on the genius level or could be. You work well with computers, science, new technology, and even astrology. This aspect is great for translating symbols into a language, which astrology is, and computer language is as well. Therefore computer programming is one skill in which you could do well. You are able to adjust well to social change and it will be something you will encounter in your life, especially at this time when it is so prevalent in society. You would make a good leader showing the way to change.

Pallas Opposition Uranus

You may encounter many situations or people who are very different from your upbringing or current belief systems, which may be a shock to you, and create an internal conflict leading to change within yourself. The bigger picture is that this is social change, and you are part of it. On the negative side you can be very rebellious and reject innovations, technology, or for change to happen in your world; or you can be a great agent for the many quick and unexpected changes that will be a part of your life. The saying "the more you change the more you stay the same" is really true.

Pallas Conjunction Neptune

You have strong intuition, and most likely are very psychic. This can manifest in other arenas such as music, art, and photography to name a few. You likely have very vivid dreams and are good at dream analysis. Psychology is also a good avenue for you as you see the bigger picture into a person's psyche. Detective work is also favored with this aspect, or at the least, you have a love of spy and intrigue movies and stories.

Pallas Sextile Neptune

You are very creative and artistic most likely in art, music, decorating, and even inventing new things. You have a knack for bringing things together seemingly out of nothing. You are adept at utilizing the creative force to bring your visions into manifestation. The strong intuition you have leads you to the answers you and others seek. You can be an oracle to others.

Pallas Square Neptune

There can be a challenge in getting what you want if you visualize negative outcomes, or are not very clear of your intentions. This can lead to confusion and even illusion or delusion. Be very positive in your thinking and you will create what you desire without all the stressful situations you envision. This can be a "get out of your own way" situation. Fear can be what trips you up. Focus on the positive to bring out positive outcomes. Be sure to articulate to others what it is you are trying to accomplish.

Pallas Trine Neptune

Photography, and creative arts will interest you and you have talents in both these arenas. Your intuition is very strong and almost telepathic. You have extreme focusing power with your mind into the psychic realms. Psychology and dream analysis are great avenues for you to pursue. You have a strong sense of justice and are also great at figuring things out and utilizing your powerful psychic skills.

Pallas Opposition Neptune

Others may be confused and not sure of your intentions. Be extra sure to explain to others what it is you are envisioning and what you really want. Learn to trust your intuition, and not second guess yourself. You do have strong intuition you just doubt yourself too much.

Pallas Conjunction Pluto

This aspect can have intense outcomes. You are very good at reading into the psyche of another and probing their behaviors. This makes you a natural psychologist or psychoanalyst. You would do well in those fields, as well as astrology, the psychic arts, and mediumship. You see many ways to transform your life and how others can theirs. Hypnotherapy would be a great avenue for you to explore.

Pallas Sextile Pluto

You have a very powerful mind capable of creating your desires, manifesting them into reality. You understand the "power" of thought, and what desire does with thought and intention: magic happens. You have a strong mind, and can see the motivations of others, without really knowing much about them. You read their intent, and you know what they are all about. Sex is a big focus for you and you love to "see" what others are all about. This is okay as long as it's not invasive, this is due to your X–ray vision that sees what others are hiding.

Pallas Square Pluto

Your strong and magnetic personality is awesome, but can get you into trouble if you're not careful. You are attracted to finding out what makes people tick, and have a natural way of probing without them knowing. This can lead to trouble and cause you to be attracted to the wrong types – the bad ones that are not good for you – or the ones who enjoy manipulation and power plays. Stop the cycle and integrate your own powerful ideals and put them to positive use.

Pallas Trine Pluto

You have natural skills into the psychology of others; you could use this in many ways, or modalities; such as hypnotherapy, psychology, psychiatry or even the psychic arts like tarot and astrology. You dig deep when looking at ways for self-improvement, you make sure you will succeed. Other areas that can be good for you are X-Ray tech, surgeon or detective.

Pallas Opposition Pluto

Others may object to your way of planning out how to completely flatten out and destroy the past, or any barriers getting in your way. This leads to power struggles and manipulations coming from both sides at different times. This aspect calls for a truce, you need to be on the same team as your opponent. Find a way for you to come to common ground and fight for the same cause. Plots of revenge are easy for you to see, but not good for you to act upon.

Pallas Conjunction ASC

This aspect gives you strong abilities in strategic planning, and your foresight is highly accurate. You are very intuitive and most likely even psychic. Your ability to see the big picture helps you out in every circumstance and people seek you out for your guidance. Areas of expertise may include, detective skills, political awareness and interest, intellectual abilities as well as healing.

Pallas Sextile ASC

Many opportunities present themselves to you due to your great foresight and planning abilities. You would make a great planner or developer and are able to invent new strategies and even prototypes. You are always politically correct in your mannerisms, statements, and temperament.

Pallas Square ASC

You may not be the most politically correct person, but you do see the big picture, it is just that you need to work on the delivery of your keen ideas and intellect. Most are way behind you in the thought process and this can frustrate you into acting or saying things others find astonishing. You may have issues with your planning and strategies in which things seem not to go right. This can be due to others or yourself getting in the way. Don't get distracted by others, you must not allow it. Proper planning prevents poor performance.

Pallas Trine ASC

You love a challenge and are great at making the strategic plan of attack to win at anything you put your mind too. Some may see you as calculating and they would be correct. This is okay, it is to your benefit, and a blessing you were born with. You have strong foresight and can see the big picture of things to come. You are highly intuitive and able to detect if anything is "wrong". Areas of expertise would be or involve; politics, fine arts, psychology, healing, and hypnosis to name a few.

Pallas Opposition ASC

Your partner, or significant other may be highly intuitive, and have Pallas traits, which include, interest in the arts, politics, seeing the big picture, and is a skilled planner or strategist. You may have many disagreements with others over planning, and organizational ideas.

Pallas Conjunction MC

Your career may involve following politics and law, such as a lawyer or judge, justice of the peace, psychology, psychics, detectives and healers of all types, especially with the mind such as hypnotherapists. You are highly skilled at planning and organizing many people and would be great in the corporate world. Pallas also is a military indicator. Any vocation which involves training and career counseling would also be good for you.

Pallas Sextile MC

You have many talents and skills for the work environment that will help you with your career. You have a strong sense of intuition, and timing, along with strategy that gets you ahead of others with similar dreams. You would do well with training, and managing others. Careers in the healing, educational, political, and military are suited for you.

Pallas Square MC

Trying to please others especially bosses and those in authority does not work well for you. This stems from your parental upbringing especially with father. You were always trying to impress and please your father, who never paid that much attention to all your efforts, making you want his approval all the more. This can be healthy in small doses and gets you motivated to do well, just don't let it rule you or put you in a bind, as they may never seem to be pleased.

Pallas Trine MC

You have such great talents and are suited for the professional field. You may have a career as a manager, or director of a large corporation, work in the legal areas, or healing fields. All these areas are beneficial for you to pursue. You can even be a counselor of many different styles, such as clinical, or even in the metaphysical areas such as the psychic fields.

Pallas Opposition MC

You may have some real issues with authority and this started with your father figure in childhood. It seems you were always trying to please him or win his approval in some way. This carried over into adulthood and thus is showing up as your boss. You have a great deal of skills, you just need the self-confidence to go forward without the approval of others. So look within in yourself and look forward to self-starting your career in your own unique way. He will come around eventually and approve.

Pallas Conjunction Vesta

You are a highly dedicated person to whatever cause you deem important. You have the ability to reach a high standing profession which stands for a higher purpose or cause. You can take sexual energy and manifest something real with this energy, this is the secret of attraction, the law of attraction, and magic. You are able to accomplish much with your broad vision and extreme dedication to purpose and cause.

Pallas Sextile Vesta

You like to fight for the underdog, or whatever cause you seek that needs attention, such as women's rights, gay rights and other revolutionary issues you feel are important. You would do well with politics and succeed in the working career world. You are a crusader for other's rights. You possess a very high degree of psychic ability, and have the devotion needed to dedicate to it.

Pallas Square Vesta

You may have a hard time with seeing the big picture in creative endeavors, as you have some blocks in your expression that need to be addressed so you can fully tap into your creative potential, which means success. You may have to watch out for being overly zealous with politics and viewpoints, as you can overdo or over reach your potential in these areas.

Pallas Trine Vesta

You are extremely talented in many areas, mainly because you have the ability to see things through to fruition. Others are not as hard working and detail oriented as you are which is why you're ahead of the game. You can be a crusader for justice and an advocate for others rights such as gay rights, women's rights etc.

Pallas Opposition Vesta

In relationships, you may feel like hot-and-cold to your partners as they have a hard time reading you and figuring out if you really like them or not. You are a devoted person to whomever you commit. There can be sexual alienation, as a result of not being close enough to feel rather than intellectualize You may be too intellectual to get to the raw emotion and sexuality that others have, due to overload in the work environment. In other words, you may be a workaholic who keeps busy just to justify not being close to another.

Pallas Conjunction Chiron

The key to your healing is in your subconscious mind. Many events in your past may have been buried or locked up in your subconscious mind. Meditation and your imagination are the key to unlocking the subconscious mind. Hypnosis would be good for you perhaps even as a career, utilizing that with psychology. The aspect of these two energies is a healing with the mind. You have a keen insight into strategic planning around the healing and health areas. There may be healing issues regarding your father or dominant parent that needs to be addressed to move forward in life.

Pallas sextile Chiron

You have quick insight into people, and can quickly see where the healing issues are within them. You have perception into healing, and would do well in the area of medical intuitive or a counselor. This aspect also favors vocational advisor, and mentorship.

Pallas Square Chiron

You can have issues about voicing your opinion on subjects that you know well. This may be a wound in your psyche regarding believing in yourself and trusting yourself. You had many instances in which someone made you doubt your knowledge and you stopped sharing that knowledge out of fear. Strive to believe in yourself, trust your inner knowing – the intuition within.

Pallas Trine Chiron

You have keen insight into the healing of those around you especially the psychological issues. You are also a natural medical intuitive and might want to explore this area. Healing professions are favored with this aspect. Other vocations include teaching, mentoring, training, and hypnosis.

Pallas Opposition Chiron

There may be arguments about how to take care of something or someone, with your significant other or others in general. Differing opinions regarding the healthcare of another such as child, aging parents etc. Conflicts within yourself about what path to take in life are evident with this aspect. Believe in yourself above all else.

VESTA

THE VESTAL VIRGIN

Goddess of the Hearth and Home. Keeper of the Flame

Key words/Themes:

As a vestal virgin, this indicates extreme devotion and dedication to a cause or a being. Consistent, devoted, dedicated, service, oriented. Can create tunnel vision with only one goal in sight. Workaholic. Periods of sexuality and celibacy. Sacrificing. Nuns, priests and the opposite sex, trade workers can all have a strong Vesta influence. Continuous. Shows our level of commitment and devotion.

Symbol: Eternal Flame

Other Name: Hestia

VESTA IN THE SIGNS

Vesta in Aries

You are very self-competitive, and once you have a focus you spend all your energy achieving that goal. Your drive and dedication is even forceful in many cases, you don't lose sight and will fight if needed to keep your goals alive and protected. You can be described as fiercely independent – be sure to be a team player once in a while. You don't sit around thinking about how to achieve a goal, you take action and get things moving; you can always go back and fix it later, so just do it. Sexually you do like to take a more dominant role initiating the act and the thrill of the chase is exciting to you.

Vesta in Taurus

Steady is the way you work, you don't change much keeping your focus and devotion strong. You are reliable and dependable in work situations and where strong devotion is needed you don't disappoint. You dedicate yourself by making sure physical needs are taken care of, the basics: food, shelter, money, so you will work hard to save the money needed for those ends. Once those are covered, you can save for later needs, down the road.

Vesta in Gemini

You're dedicated to keeping your word, and preserving the teachings by re-telling the stories of the past. Mental focus is very strong in this sign placement. Service may involve two different areas or concepts to which you have committed. Teaching is a role very well suited for this sign, especially in the language, reading and writing departments. There may be a strong devotion to your siblings. A sibling may be in the clergy.

Vesta in Cancer

Family and home traditions are highly important to you and you dedicate yourself to them. Mother may have a very strong influence over your life. Spirituality is strong here, as you take on the life role of parent: mother or father to the world. Sexually, you must feel a connection and be devoted or it is not going to be fulfilling to you.

Vesta in Leo

Creativity, and your ambitions are what you are dedicated to fulfilling. It as if your soul's purpose is to create, and with your huge vision and insight you are driven to success. When in love you are extremely devoted to that person. You are very protective and devoted to your children as they are your creations as well. Sexuality is highly important as a joy to be had, which keeps the creativity and life force strong in you.

Vesta in Virgo

This sign may be the home to Vesta. You are very committed to work and service, as they are your calling. It is a form of self-sacrifice, and you may literally devote your work to a higher calling as in the clergy, or being a nun. Self-denial in sex as in celibacy or the exact opposite, high sexuality with multiple partners may take place.

Vesta in Libra

You are very dedicated and devoted to partnerships. You have high regard for your partner. Co-dependency may be an issue with this placement. Be sure not to forsake your own identity and purpose by giving all to your partner. You like being with your other half and may work with him or her. Keeping harmony is a spiritual calling to which you hear and respond. Sexually, you can be very accommodating, achieving balance and harmony between both of you. There may be role reversal.

Vesta in Scorpio

Your spiritual calling is sexual transformation, to explore the hidden and the taboos of sexuality and society. You are deeply devoted to the person to whom you commit, in 'til-death-do-us-part style of dedication. You go to the depths in all your pursuits, healing is the goal, leaving no stone unturned. You protect what is sacred and love the occult, seeking power to heal and transform. Sexually, tantric practices relate to this sign placement of Vesta.

Vesta in Sagittarius

Your belief system or religion is paramount, and a huge calling you need to explore and devote yourself to in this lifetime. This is the placement for priests, nuns, and other types of philosophers including professors at a college. This placement also relates to metaphysics and spiritual devotion. There may be many beliefs or taboos related to sexuality depending on the spiritual view point. Rituals and ceremonies are important for you to practice.

Vesta in Capricorn

You are devoted to work, and achieving success and status. You take on heavy amounts of responsibility, and thrive best in an organized and structured environment. Governmental jobs are a good example, police, and the military. You have long and strong endurance to get the tasks done, and would make a great manager of others. Sexually this can be abstinence or the extreme opposite as Capricorn is often all or nothing.

Vesta in Aquarius

You have strong dedication to your friends, and the groups to which you belong. You are a true humanitarian and love people and mother earth. You can dedicate yourself to many social causes that benefit humanity. Sexuality is more progressive and can be open to casual encounters or with friends.

Vesta in Pisces

Spirituality is what you devote yourself to, a higher power. You have a deep love of the psychic and the mystical. You don't just believe – you know that there is more to life than the physical and mundane. You believe in strong service to humanity through spirituality, and doing good. Karma is a strong word for you that you live by. Sexually you need to feel that you are soulmates to have a strong dedication and devotion to your partner. You may also feel that you have "many partners, or soul mates".

VESTA IN THE HOUSES

Vesta in the First house

You're a very devoted, dedicated and focused individual. You tend to be very serious and hard working toward anything the evokes feelings of devotion within you. Commitment is a strong word you live by. Perfection can be the goal with Vesta here.

Vesta in the Second House

You are dedicated to providing substance and all the survival needs for yourself and your family. You may seem over focused on this area but it is what is needed. Vesta can be related to money as in "invested", and this can manifest literally into investing into stocks etc.

Vesta in the Third house

Your neighborhood is a value to you and you may seem to be the one to keep things together as a community. Serving on a community panel or board, or HOA committee would be a good outlet for you. You may feel responsible for your siblings, and you are devoted to them. Writing is a great focus for you to get your thoughts out. Your communication style may be very quiet or not easily understood.

Vesta in the Fourth house

You may be the one who has to take care of the whole family. You are devoted to your family whether it is biological or an extended family. Spirituality is strong in the home, and it is a divine place, your retreat from the world, a sanctuary. Meditation is important and focus on spiritual matters. Having a fireplace, or some sort of altar is important as Vesta is keeper of the flame.

Vesta in the Fifth house

You are dedicated to your creations, especially your children. Your personal creativity is very important but this can lead to sexual repression if you use all of your creative force on hobbies, it leaves your sex life wanting.

Vesta in the Sixth house

Your life is dedicated to service, it is your calling. You love to work, help, give, and you are dedicated to your job. You may have interest in serving the church or another belief system as in becoming a priest or nun. Healing is an avenue you may dedicate yourself to, as well as good health.

Vesta in the Seventh house

You're so devoted to your partner, it's like you were born to be with each other. You may even sacrifice your identity a little in doing so, just watch to see that it does not become co-dependency in which you lose yourself totally. You love doing things for your significant other, you may even spend your day doing so. This is a good placement for working with your spouse.

Vesta in the Eighth house

You are dedicated to deep spiritual transformation, sexuality is one of the ways you do this. You have interest in psychology, karma, and the occult, you dedicate your life to research in the hidden areas, the taboos. By diving in deep you transform your life through catharsis. Sex may be intense with one or with multiple partners. Tantric practices will help your spiritual journey. You have a deep honor of your ancestors and to people who are on the other side of the veil. Investing in stocks is also a manifestation of Vesta in this house.

Vesta in the Ninth house

You are dedicated to your belief system, and if it is a religion, you devote your life to serving that religion and ultimately God. You may also be drawn to other spiritual belief systems such as paganism or esotericism in which you do the same, and devote your life or a major part of it, to your belief system. It may even be a philosophy or higher education that you invest your time in. Vesta likes rituals with an altar, and candles you may try this in honor of Vesta as the ninth house is about rituals.

Vesta in the Tenth house

Your career is what you devote your time and energy to. You may be a workaholic, as you spend much more time at work than with your family. There is a strong need and desire to succeed but also a strong loyalty to your career, job, boss or purpose in life. It's as though you have this higher calling to do your chosen career. There is a spiritual purpose in this even if it is not apparent on the outside.

Vesta in the Eleventh house

You are devoted to your friends and the groups to which you belong. This is a perfect placement and example of someone in a secret society, such as the Freemasons, or Rosicrucians. It can even be your local astrology society. Friends are highly important to you. You also can manifest your wishes hopes and dreams by creating an altar, with pictures of what you desire. Activate it daily or at least look at it for a few moments every day for best benefit.

Vesta in the Twelfth house

You are dedicated to spiritual causes and pursuits. You may devote your time to helping the needy, or the sick. Vesta likes being behind the scenes, so this placement is very good, you like to serve unnoticed or selflessly. You may keep your personal devotions secret. Past lives were dedicated to spirituality, and the divine. You may have been one of the Vestal Virgins.

VESTA IN ASPECT

Vesta Conjunction Sun

You are very focused and committed to your purpose in life. You will work diligently and with all the devotion in your heart to carry things through. This may mean that you are a little self-sacrificing at times which will pay off in the long run. You identify with having a cause or destiny that you came into this lifetime to fulfill, and you have the tools needed to be successful. Sexually you may identify yourself either as a chaste person, or one who is devoted to all, but no one in particular. This can mean you want to give of yourself (sexually) to many without having an ego attachment involved, like an open relationship. Archetypes; nun, priest, prostitute, celibate, nymph, workaholic.

Vesta Sextile Sun

You may be called an over-achiever as you can accomplish much with your steady dedication to work. Work for you is devotion, and hard work, it pays off, as you have the work ethic that is needed for success in your endeavors. This makes you a great career person. You are very devoted to any person or cause to which you commit.

Vesta Square Sun

There are many challenges that come up in regards to your career and what your parent's wishes for you may have been. This can cause you to be at odds with yourself over what you want to do with your life. Are you really committed? Do you want to dedicate that much to your cause or purpose? You can achieve all you desire, it will just take a little more hard work than it does for most other people, until you do commit and focus your energies – then you will be unstoppable. You may have two different ideals that you want to commit to, but can only commit to one.

Vesta Trine Sun

Focus and dedication describe you and your actions. This is why you are very successful in your enterprises. You know how to work hard, and you have the commitment to stay with your chosen project. Success is yours and it was earned. There are many areas of talents or vocations in which you would be great: healing, investments, stocks, big business, clergy or spiritual paths.

Vesta Opposition Sun

You will learn at some point in your life the meaning of devotion, dedication and commitment as Vesta is opposing your identity, meaning there are some major lessons to learn and to integrate these values into your personal life, and incorporate them into your work habits. You may have some relationship issues, with the main issue being your inability to devote and commit yourself to the other person. Once you learn the importance of dedication and focus on one person or ideal this will become balanced and integrated into your life.

Vesta Conjunction Moon

You have deep feelings and are very emotionally connected and devoted to those you love. This may even mean some sacrifice on your part. You may give up something to stay with family or those whom you care for. Memories, and deep feelings of the past are some of your greatest rewards in your life. Family is something you hold dear to your heart, and to which you are very dedicated.

Vesta Sextile Moon

You have an excellent memory, especially around family and the past, and you treasure those fond memories as if they were gold. You are a dedicated person to anyone you care about, especially family, and those you trust. Career may involve care giving of others.

Vesta Square Moon

You may have a fear of getting close to others, especially intimate relationships. There may have been difficulty with mother or early family situations where you did not feel like the rest of the family: alienated. It may be difficult at first to commit to others and trust, but in time you will integrate this into your life.

Vesta Trine Moon

You would make a great nurse, caretaker or parent, as you are very emotionally dedicated and focused on those you care about. In relationships you have an easy time getting to know others on a deep emotional level, and even in intimate relations you are easily devoted, and committed to that person.

Vesta Opposition Moon

Relationships that require focus, and commitment may be hard for you, unless you feel like they are worthy of your dedication and commitment. You may not have had relationships early on that taught you the value and meaning of caring, and devoting yourself to another. This can make it difficult for you to connect with others on an emotional level. There may be a fear of getting too close, or intimate. You could have even been taught it was bad to get too close.

Vesta conjunction Mercury

You have a very strong mind that can focus on the minute details, and keep the concentration going for long periods of time. You can even seem obsessive to others as you don't lose your train of thought. You are good at keeping your word as you feel your word is your honor.

Vesta Sextile Mercury

You can excel in areas of research, or any technology field that requires strong powers of concentration. Writing is also a good field for you as you would be very detailed, and go deeply into the subject with strong dedication.

Vesta Square Mercury

There can be problems with focus and concentration in getting tasks completed, or with your memory. Communication can also be an issue, with words not being articulated, and thoughts being unfocused and confusing to the other person. Be sure to be clear in what you say, and ask if they understand.

Vesta Trine Mercury

You can excel as an expert in what you choose to focus on, as you leave no stone unturned in your research. You may have in-depth knowledge in certain fields of interest, and retain this information in your memory bank.

Vesta Opposition Mercury

There can be communication problems or restrictions in your speaking as you choose to be silent unless you really need to say something. You can have a hard time concentrating or keeping your focus, as it quickly diverts to other areas.

Vesta Conjunction Venus

You are very dedicated to the one you love, to the exclusion of all else. This is especially good for committed relationships and marriage. You also love to work and serve others as a way of truly giving of yourself. You expect the same treatment for yourself, and are most likely going to marry for life.

Vesta Sextile Venus

You have an active sex life, and you are in love with the one you are with or it's not at all. Love and commitment go hand in hand in your book, and that is what you expect in return. You will have fulfillment in your love life.

Vesta Square Venus

You may have a question of, what do I want in a relationship? Love and beauty or the sensible dutiful spouse? Religious reasons may confuse you and your judgment in relationships and your sex life, there may be a conflict there that needs examining. Do you have to marry a virgin? Do you have to be a virgin? What about my sexual desires? Examine closely what your beliefs are and what the conflict is. Are you okay with open relationships? These are all scenario's surrounding this aspect in your chart-life. Celibacy versus passionate sexuality.

Vesta Trine Venus

One result of this aspect is that your investments will pay off and bring you money. This is what you are invested in, it will bring you what you value: money, love, abundance. This is a very good aspect for love life, falling in love with the person who is dedicated to you. It can also be a monetary good thing as you made a wise choice in your in–vest–ment.

Vesta Opposition Venus

There may be problems with your values and your desires conflicting with commitments, and dedication. You may want to be free in relationships, and non-committal, or swing back and forth between the two. You may have issues with your beliefs about sex and what you desire sexually. You may want to be celibate until married, or want to marry a virgin, however you have very lusty desires which confuse you and your values. The question you need to ask is: Is this your own value judgments or your parents? If it is your parents and your upbringing then you need to look again at your real beliefs and make some changes.

Vesta Conjunction Mars

You have a high amount of drive and ambition when it comes to something to which you are devoted. You have a great deal of focus and drive to accomplish anything you set your desires on. This can relate to you being a hard and dedicated worker, with lots of energy and ambition. You don't feel as if your responsibilities are a burden to you, others may even see you as a fanatical worker. This placement is good for any job that requires long hours, devotion to a cause, and high amounts of concentration.

Vesta Sextile Mars

You seem to have a boundless energy, with long lasting stamina and a desire for precision. You are able to streamline your energies into productive results. You would do well with getting the job done in a very efficient and timely manner. Any skill that takes dedication and lots of practice to accomplish would be something you can achieve, such as playing the guitar, a sport or even sewing. These talents can seem effortless to you, where others would not have the patience or attention span to keep on going.

Vesta Square Mars

Focus may be hard for you as you get distracted easily, and need to have action going on at all times. This makes it hard for you to accomplish things that take patience, focus, and dedication. This is not attention deficit disorder, you don't have that from this aspect. It simply may be difficult for you to do things that take precision and sustained focus. There may be indifference or anger towards those who do not have the same beliefs as you or share the same devotion(s). Sexually this may be a fear of intimacy or guilt regarding sex, review your beliefs about sex and see where this came from.

Vesta Trine Mars

You could excel at sports or any skill that requires great focus and energy. This aspect would favor a military career. You are a self-determined individual, who will make sure that things get done. You have a huge drive to accomplish your goals.

Vesta Opposition Mars

Relationships may be difficult for you until you commit and dedicate yourself to another. Vesta wants complete devotion and intimacy on a close level. Mars just wants to have a fling, with no commitment involved. This can be a fear of getting close to another a fear of intimacy that you need to examine to find out what the root cause is and what can you do about it.

Vesta Conjunction Juno

You like being in a long term committed relationship, such as marriage. You will be devoted and spiritually connected to your marriage partner, indicating that you will be together for the long haul, totally dedicated to one another.

Vesta Sextile Juno

You are so devoted to your significant other that others see it and see how well you get along. Rituals and ceremonies will be important in your love life, this may come from your partner more than from you, but it will actually help keep you together longer. This aspect favors long term marriage that is harmonious and sexually satisfying for both.

Vesta Square Juno

There may be conflict in your relationships regarding time spent away from each other versus time spent together. You will have to make sure you don't alienate your other half, while working and devoting time to your cause. This will cause the marriage stress. The challenge is to balance alone time with together time to keep the flames of passion going.

Vesta Trine Juno

You will share the same devotion and dedication to ideals and or religion with your marriage partner. This aspect favors a happy relationship/marriage that is long lasting and the two of you are dedicated to each other. Investments involving your spouse or significant other should turn out well and profitable.

Vesta Opposition Juno

You may have difficulty dealing with relationships. The problem may be differing belief systems and traditions, as well as cultural rituals that are completely at odds with one another. Other issues can revolve around being too self-absorbed, or too busy to spend quality time with each other. This can alienate each other in the relationship. Work towards sharing time with each other and perhaps find a cause or charity you can both agree on spending time to improve the cause.

Vesta Conjunction Jupiter

You can be extremely devoted to your religion, or belief system. You love spending time dedicated to your cause or vision, and are always in search of the truth. This aspect favors careers such as politician, clergy, marriage officiant, and counselor.

Vesta Sextile Jupiter

You should experience good pay through your career, or job as you are a dedicated employee, and hard worker – the devotion pays off. You have great spiritual concepts, and a belief system that brings you greater opportunities, due to your strong devotion to a cause or belief.

Vesta Square Jupiter

You may be at odds with family philosophies or religious teachings, as they do not resonate with you. You may see flaws in their teachings or beliefs that you can't seem to just ignore. You will most likely have to find your own life philosophy to live by, which is the most important thing anyway.

Vesta Trine Jupiter

You are a very devoted person to whatever cause or belief system you have. It is highly important to you to believe in a higher power. You have a great positive outlook on life that is very sincere as you truly do resonate with your beliefs. You have a great mind that loves to learn and expand, encouraging you to want to learn more and more about your philosophy of life. You may travel for religious purposes, like to a foreign country to learn about their ways and rituals.

Vesta Opposition Jupiter

You have to learn not to overdo your beliefs, what this means is not becoming too involved in your religion or belief system that you don't look to new ideas, or ideologies that may be counter to current thought. This can be a conflict of beliefs versus logic or science, or religion versus science. This may show up significantly in your relationships.

Vesta Conjunction Saturn

You are a very hard working individual who has the capacity and dedication to see things through until they manifest successfully. You are very devoted to the work and service you give, and highly responsible – almost to a fault. Be careful that your dedication to your career and calling does not interfere with your personal relationships and cause alienation.

Vesta Sextile Saturn

Your self-discipline and hard work will pay off especially where career is concerned. You have the capacity for managerial work, and can work long hours. You love being duty bound with all these obligations, it doesn't feel like a burden to you, as you really enjoy the hard work and you do get satisfaction from it.

Vesta Square Saturn

There may be some challenges in your life regarding your work life, delays in getting your career started or a promotion. Obstacles that distract you from your career or work may be due to your belief system or dedication to other interests that cause you to be distracted and to pull away. Be careful that you don't ignore your relationship needs due to career demands.

Vesta Trine Saturn

With your acclaimed sense of self-discipline you can achieve much in your life, especially around career goals. Your devotion and hard work – which never loses focus – keeps you in the limelight amongst your superiors. Your boss does take notice, and even if it does take a while to get to the top, you will. This aspect gives you a serious personality especially in the career arena. Be sure not to dress too drab, in dark conservative clothes. Professional is one thing, but you need to have some style as well. You would do well in jobs or careers that relate to the elderly.

Vesta Opposition Saturn

There may be delays in your career choice due to other obligations and duties you had to focus on. There may have been just too much to pursue a career that would have taken all your time away from your other concerns. You will have to learn to balance your time spent at work versus time with your family and home life to have a pleasant, meaningful relationship.

Vesta Conjunction Uranus

You are a non-conformist type individual, who has your own unique sense of what and who you will dedicate yourself to, on a personal level and a belief system level, including religion. Sexually you may have a hard time committing to one person and may be attracted to many very different archetypes. Unusual and strange is good for you as you get bored by everyday mundane events and situations. Your love life is very colorful.

Vesta Sextile Uranus

You have a talent for being innovative especially in the science and even occult areas of life. With strong focusing abilities you are able to see the patterns, as a language, that speaks volumes to you. You would be great at astrology, and even working with computer technology, programming etc., as it is written in a language in which you could easily understand and excel.

Vesta Square Uranus

You don't like conforming to the customs and rituals of the past, whether it be family tradition or religious beliefs of the family, you are sure to rebel. You have a hard time keeping your focus and concentration as your early life was disrupted so much that you almost gave up trying. Anything you were committed too was either taken away suddenly or radically changed so that you did not trust what you were committing to any longer. Commitment issues are what has resulted from your childhood. With this knowledge you can redefine and change this issue now that you know the cause.

Vesta Trine Uranus

You would do well to study shamanistic practices, and any

new or innovative spiritual techniques. New Age beliefs appeal to you, especially around rituals, magic, astrology, and tantric practices. Science and technology are also good subjects in which you can excel. Trust in your intuition, as it is very strong, it comes in the form of just knowing, and through meditation and ritual.

Vesta Opposition Uranus

You can seem to be a rebel in many instances, as you like to change up the routine that has been established by others. Conforming to a cause or belief system may be very difficult for you as you are trying to invent new rituals, systems, and devoting yourself to new causes. Many see you as strange and unusual. Relationships can be difficult as it is hard for you to commit, as you want adventure and excitement and don't like routine and boring stability. Sexually you can be adventurous always looking for something new and exciting.

Vesta Conjunction Neptune

You have a strong sense of direction in the spiritual paths and have a strong knowing psychically about your spiritual path and direction. You may utilize this energy for the arts, and/or music, which could lead to becoming a very talented musician. You give selflessly of yourself to a greater cause.

Vesta Sextile Neptune

You possess a very creative imagination and have the devotion and focus needed to develop and perfect your skills in the arts and or music. Spirituality is a high focus for you, as you easily see the bigger picture, and spiritually and instinctively know the path you should take.

Vesta Square Neptune

There may be some confusion for you in your spiritual path, stemming from conflicting beliefs. Your spiritual teachings from an early age may be in conflict with your current beliefs or sexual practices, and lifestyle. Integrate your true spiritual self and then you will have no question or concerns regarding sexuality as you will just "know".

Vesta Trine Neptune

The spiritual path seems right for you as you possess many natural skills in the psychic arena, as well as in psychic healing, such as reiki. You would make a natural and excellent reiki master with this aspect in your chart. You are a natural "shaman". The fine arts and music will most likely appeal to you, and you would also do well to pursue those interests.

Vesta Opposition Neptune

You may have some confusion regarding your religious upbringing, and the beliefs that were instilled in you at a young age may have cause you to become confused by what you are devoted to spiritually. This may relate to sexual confusion as well, based again on your belief system, and what you are supposed to be devoted to. This can cause problems with relationships, and commitment issues, that need to be addressed so that you can have a healthy, committed relationship.

Vesta Conjunction Pluto

You are a very powerful individual and have great dedication and devotion to your spiritual pursuits and causes. You can affect the masses of people with your causes, and create long lasting change for the good with this aspect. Research, science, inventing things or ideas is likely to be a strong interest in you. Investments and the stock market would also serve you well.

Vesta Sextile Pluto

You find it stimulating to do research into the unknown and have the curiosity and drive to create something or discover something of mass appeal. Intuitive ideas come to you as you get deeper into your search as it is part of the process. Vesta seeks a deep and meaningful sexual experience with this aspect of Pluto, which is healthy, do not feel guilty over your sexual power.

Vesta Square Pluto

You may have a strange fear or obsession with death. Be sure not to become overly isolated and shut off from the outside world, as it can lead to actual fear of the public or some paranoia. There may be sexual guilt and as a result, obsession over it, or a phobia. Learn all you can about sexuality so you do not have those issues in your relationships. Sexual dominance can be a manifestation of this aspect.

Vesta Trine Pluto

You have a strong sense of self, knowing what you believe in, and you have the devotion and dedication to manifest what you desire. This is a powerful aspect and when you know how to use this power or skill you have great power to manifest what you desire. Read up on the law of attraction books, and creative visualization, with this aspect you are a powerhouse.

Vesta Opposition Pluto

This aspect can have heavy issues with sexuality, if there was any sort of abuse or power and control with sex, this can cause phobias, and many psychological issues. However, a healthy state is where there is balance between the sexual urge and your devotion, and using it to truly empower yourself and the other person. A great transformational healing can take place. Tantra could be very good, when you have a healthy outlook on sexuality.

Vesta Conjunction Ascendant

You are a dedicated and devoted individual. You have strong values and beliefs and will sacrifice your personal desires until all your obligations are met. Spirituality is highly important to you, and is part of your everyday life. Focus is a strength you have, and you accomplish much due to this quality. Rituals and tradition are of interest to you. Sexuality is highly important and is seen as a spiritual connection to the divine, and sharing that with another individual is very rewarding so you keep it very sacred.

Vesta Sextile Ascendant

You are a committed and sincere person to all you meet. You truly are of service with no thought of something in return. Giving and sharing is a trait you possess. Others may not understand you or think you may have something ulterior in your motives – this is not true. You have a strong sense of duty and responsibility.

Vesta Square Ascendant

You may feel uncomfortable around others that don't share the same values, and standards that you have. Harsh or brash people who have no sense of responsibility confuse and upset your balance. Others may see you as too conservative and overly focused. You may need to let your wild side shine through once in a while.

Vesta Trine Ascendant

You have a knack for knowing how to organize and get things done. It may be your power of focus and your high commitment that prevails and accomplishes major tasks. You have a strong sense of duty and are dedicated to whatever cause you decide worthy of pursuing.

Vesta Opposition Ascendant

You attract highly devoted and committed people for relationships. Your partner will be dedicated and very giving to you. Commitment is strong in your personal relationships. You may marry after age 30 most likely at age 36.

Vesta Conjunction MC

You may be called a workaholic by close friends and family. It's just that you are very dedicated and devoted to your career, it's like a baby that needs constant attention. Be sure to balance your time at home with your family. You are known for sacrificing your own needs for the good of the job, or company. The good thing is that this pays off well.

Vesta Sextile MC

You have many skills and there are many people behind you supporting your efforts of your career ideals and goals. You will be known as a competent, focused and committed person in your chosen field.

Vesta Trine MC

Dedication, devotion and personal sacrifice has put you where you are in your career. You should be successful as you know how to make the difference and keep the focus to the tasks at hand. This ensures your success.

Vesta Opposition MC

Family is highly important to you and where your commitment and dedication lies. Be sure to balance your time between career and family; don't neglect the career for the family, as it will backfire in the long run. A fireplace in the home is good for this placement. You sacrifice a great deal for your family.

Vesta Conjunction Chiron

You are a highly evolved spiritual person who is dedicated to helping humanity, and you are a natural healer, teacher, trainer and coach. You are devoted to healing and mentoring those in need. You may be considered a shaman, and or a spiritual teacher by many. Finding your path and sticking to it is the key for your success, whether you do traditional healing or more alternative.

Vesta Sextile Chiron

Service and devotion to a cause is a strong trait you have. You are extremely focused on whatever cause to which you have devoted yourself. This aspect shows interest in the higher spiritual disciplines considered "new age" or spiritual in nature. You have a talent for spiritual, and healing work, so make the most of it.

Vesta Trine Chiron

You are a highly evolved spiritual teacher, and your mission is to teach, train or coach, and mentor those who need your specific type of knowledge. You may be called a guru by some. This is a very positive aspect, showing many special talents, don't hide them from the world, and share them wisely.

Vesta Opposition Chiron

There may be conflicts with others regarding your spiritual beliefs and practices. Others may see you as strange and "not like them". This is great. You're not like them. Good. Now you just need to find the right person as there is one that will be the perfect partner for you. You will feel much more centered and content around age thirty six.

⚷

CHIRON

WOUNDED HEALER, MASTER TEACHER

Chiron was the wounded healer, with a wound that would not heal. Zeus felt sorry for him and put him in the constellation as Sagittarius. He was a master astrologer and teacher of many of the arts, medicine, healing etc.

Key Words/themes:

Shaman, master healer, doctor, mentor, teacher, astrologer. Where we have a wound by house, sign, aspect. Placement gives us clues as to how to cope with and heal, or overcome the wound. Once we master the wound we become the advocate for healing, and educating.

CHIRON IN THE SIGNS

⚷

Chiron in Aries

Your quest is to be the hero or heroine in your own life according to your own ideals of what a hero is. You have to establish your own rules in life being brave enough to go against the social norms and be the pioneer and maverick – you've got to be you. Getting over shyness, and being overly cordial without regard for yourself is the lesson you must master.

Chiron in Taurus

Your journey is to feel security with yourself first and foremost, and not feel you need designer labels, clothing, and jewelry, or the latest shoe's to feel that you are of value to society. Those things are all great and okay to have when you already feel inside that they don't make you who you are. Survival issues may be an issue you had to overcome: poverty, loss, and heavy experiences; know you need to learn to relax and enjoy the comforts and joys of life.

Chiron in Gemini

You will need to overcome your fear of communicating with others. You may have been wounded by the words of others and have a deep fear of talking to others or sharing your ideas and concepts as you may have been labeled in the past. Once you learn how to communicate with many, and in crowds, your words can heal like no other. You would do well in any of the communication fields and counseling as well.

Chiron in Cancer

Your feelings are very sensitive and you tend to hide in your safe shell all too often. Chiron in Cancer means you need to heal those deep emotions that keep you secure when healed. Then you will be the advocate and healer for all those souls who need an alternate parent or nurturer.

Chiron in Leo

You started out this life with a bruised ego, making you very insecure about your unique talents and creative pursuits. You may have been made to feel you have no talents. You need to heal those thoughts and get on with your hobbies, instruments, or whatever creative field you have can potentially heal others through your creative outlet. By holding back you may be blocking someone down the road who could have used your inspiration.

Chiron in Virgo

In your youth you may have been made to feel as if you were not good enough, and that if you only tried harder you would get the approval you sought. This has caused you to become a perfectionist at best and a critic at worst. Take it easy on yourself and realize you already are perfect. Your life and those around you will change dramatically. Having this wound and insecurity deep down may have made you interested in the healing arts or fields. You should pursue those fields.

Chiron in Libra

Fairness and equality are big issues in your life, always looking to make everything even and fair for all. This is very hard to do and you have to learn to let go and let God, or karma take its place as well in many situations. This placement of Chiron gives you interest in social issues, justice and relationship equality. Your relationships are where you need to focus and learn how to be a couple and an individual. Counseling is a natural healing talent for you especially couples counseling.

Chiron in Scorpio

With Chiron in this sign you have deep interest in healing, research, and sexuality. Many of you will be surgeons, nurses, caretakers, shamans, tantric teachers, mortgage brokers, or work in the morgue. This placement is not for the weak. This gives you a brave soul who wants to dig to the ends of earth to find the reason for the wound, and how to heal that wound. You most likely had to heal a deep wound from birth over which you had no control. Solving the mystery of it all is your quest, healing others is your destiny.

Chiron in Sagittarius

You have a strong placement of Chiron in Sagittarius, they are representations of each other. Chiron's traits as a maverick, shaman, healer and teacher as well as philosopher are all great ways to describe you. You may have to heal the belief systems you were taught from your parents and society, as you can't just accept their word and you will explore the world first as a rebel, looking for truth – your own truth. You will find all the flaws and actual illusions you were taught and replace them with your own philosophies, and healing ways.

Chiron in Capricorn

You have a deep need to feel useful to others – in other words valued and needed. This makes you work very hard assuming many responsibilities, some of which may not have been a choice in your childhood, but you were relied on to take over and do. You are healing the wound of not feeling needed or wanted, whether from this life or a previous one. You love structure and traditional forms of healing. There may be healing to do with the father or father figures in your life.

Chiron in Aquarius

You had a rebel streak in you as a youth, as you are here to break tradition and start new trends. You are progressive and love alternative ways of doing things especially around healing modalities. You are also healing the past, in that you had many broken dreams and let-downs in past lives, now you are the progressive healer with big dreams and wishes for humanity. Chiron in this sign favors astrology, as he was a master astrologer.

Chiron in Pisces

You are keenly intuitive and very imaginative, and this leads you to a spiritual life. Your biggest concerns really are spiritual in nature, becoming a better person, healing those in need, and attuning yourself to the highest spiritual vibrations. You have interest in the law of attraction, creative visualizations, and will become the master and teacher of these subjects. This placement is good for shamans, reiki masters and psychics.

CHIRON IN THE HOUSES

⚷

Chiron in the First House

With Chiron in the house of your personality and personal life you are very Chiron like, a teacher, trainer, coach, mentor, healer, shaman, guru, and even astrologer. These subjects interest you enough to become one of the archetypes of them. You may have had a wound to your ego, or even your physical body that needs healing and may feel like a lifelong quest that you have had to deal with.

Chiron in the Second House

You may make your money through a healing modality, or as a teacher, mentor or astrologer. You value healing, education and mentoring others, and leaving them an ideal to strive for in their lives. Spiritual values are important to you. You may have lessons to learn around the value of money, and this can be a major wound you need to heal. Many took a vow of poverty in previous lives, if this sounds like you, then it is time to renounce that vow and recommit to a vow of prosperity, as that is a highly spiritual vibration.

Chiron in the Third House

There may be a wound you have with a sibling that needs healing. This wound could have started in a past life, and the resolution may happen in this lifetime. You may need to mentor and teach your siblings. You may have a quest to learn as much about healing, as you can and then to teach and share this knowledge with as many as you can.

Chiron in the Fourth House

Family is an important part of your life although it did not come without baggage and many issues that need(ed) healing. Usually we start out with our dysfunctional family and have to go through a healing process, once healed we become the teacher of the same wound. What did you have to move through to survive your family life? Have you healed this and moved forward? By healing this you will feel an inner sense of security that no one can shake.

Chiron in the Fifth House

You need to heal your inner child. You have the ability to heal others through your personal creativity. Whether it is singing, music, art, acting, or whatever your modality of creativity is, it can be used for healing many, as they will either follow in your footsteps, or find healing through the inspiration you bring. You may have been down-played in your childhood or told not to pursue your dreams, wounding your ego. You must master your talents and share them. Chiron used music in his healing arts teachings.

Chiron in the Sixth House

This placement is great for those who want to be healers, as it is something that comes naturally to you. You may have or had many health issues, that needed healing, and as a result you become the advocate for those issues that you once had. Nutritionist, acupuncture, energy healing and exercise are all excellent for you as a lifestyle or career. Food sensitivities may lead you to specialized diets such as vegan, vegetarian, gluten free, organic etc.

Chiron in the Seventh House

Healing is accomplished through your relationships, and because of your relationships. This is a mirroring of the shadow side of yourself which needs to be examined. As you project your healing or needs on others they manifest as relationships that need fixing. Once you have transformed this and healed yourself your partnerships will be miraculously better. You may marry a healer, a doctor or a shaman, or someone who has Chiron very prominent in their chart.

Chiron in the Eighth House

You have had a life of many deep transformational experiences, ranging from death of loved ones at an early age, to having some type of abuse or extreme control at the hands of another. Many with this placement experience paranormal experiences in their lifetime that opens them up to wanting to research more in this area. Sex and sexuality often needs to be healed. Career choices can be tantric or sex therapists, adult industry, or psychologist, detective or mortician.

Chiron in the Ninth House

This is an excellent position for Chiron to be in, and you may even say this is his home. You are a teacher, trainer, a coach and a sage. You are a great mentor to others, a guide who can lead the way, through your knowledge. Religion and spirituality are important to you. There may be a wound that creates a quest for the truth, regarding the meaning of life itself.

Chiron in the Tenth House

You may have some healing to do with your father or your dominant parent. This translates into authority figures and issues with them in adulthood. You may feel a strong need to prove yourself worthy of success to your parent(s). Career becomes a way for you to heal yourself and bring up your self-worth and esteem. You would do well in careers related to healing, mentoring, teaching, and astrology.

Chiron in the Eleventh House

A need to belong and be part of the group is highly important to you. You want to contribute to the group and the world at large in the bigger picture. This makes you a little different and maybe eccentric as you want to create and invent a new future, something to be known for. You will no doubt bring many great changes to society, by being a part of society and contributing to it.

Chiron in the Twelfth House

You have a strong need for retreat, and isolation to an extent in order to heal your inner wound, as you may have no idea what the cause of this wound is, or where it came from, the only place to look is inward, inside yourself. It may have cause in a past life, whatever the cause it is very subconscious and needs to be brought to light in order to understand and heal. This can manifest in you working in large institutions, like hospitals or prisons, where seclusion is the norm. Interests include healing, nursing, counseling, rehabilitation, drug or alcohol recovery counselor, and psychic and energy healer. You may have been a nun or monk, in a past life or a thieving vagabond that made you end up in prison.

CHIRON IN ASPECT

⚷

Chiron Conjunction Sun

You have a deep need to find yourself, your own identity. You need to feel secure from the inside, that you are worthy of appreciation, and you are a valued person in society. You may have been wounded very deeply at a young age, triggering this quest to be "somebody." Projection on to others can be an issue with this aspect that does not serve you. Go within yourself and heal, then you will become the healer of others and you will shine as a valued person in society. You have to be real with yourself and in touch with your inner self before outer world success can come in, inner fulfilment will follow.

Chiron Sextile Sun

You have special talents and you need to use them. You will get over the initial fear of inadequacy once you take the first step and go for it – "just do it"– take the chance. You will excel in whatever you do, don't be afraid of success or toot your own horn. This aspect is giving you the opportunity to shine. You will be well known for your creative and artistic talents, as well as healing, teaching and mentoring skills.

Chiron Square Sun

You have issues with your own self-worth that needs to be healed. There may have been no recognition from your parents. They may have been too busy for you and as a result you did not get the attention you deserved. This created low self-esteem and a feeling of not deserving. Nothing can be further from the truth. You are a valued part of society and the world, and you need to shine your inner light for all to see. Take the challenge and get out there and show the world who you are.

Chiron Trine Sun

You have a special talent or gift to bring to society. It may be in the form of healing, teaching, mentoring, or a creative and artistic talent. You will do things in your own way usually breaking tradition, you may be seen as a rebel until it catches on in mainstream society. You would most likely do well with astrology as well.

Chiron Opposition Sun

You will attract relationships that will help you bring out the real you, and heal any inner wounds left over from childhood. If you did not get the attention you deserved as a child, relationships will be problematic until this is resolved, and what is needed before relationships can be healthy. One issue this aspect brings is projection of your needs onto your partner. This is not healthy in that you have to accept all issues and faults as your own and not to project them onto your partner. Once this is done you will have exciting, fulfilling relationships, better than you would have ever imagined.

Chiron Conjunction Moon

You have a hard time emoting and expressing your inner feelings, as this was not expressed in childhood. Your mother may have not expressed her emotions or was unavailable physically or emotionally. As a result you may be empathic as you are very sensitive to what others are thinking or feeling about you. Once you open up your emotions and become vulnerable to others the positive traits will become prevalent. You make a great counselor, mentor, and teacher for those in need of healing their emotions, and early childhood experiences. Care giving in many forms is good for you, and those you assist.

Chiron Sextile Moon

You make a great counselor, and care giver with this harmonious aspect. Your soothing personality makes others feel at ease, and welcome in your presence. Your mother was soothing and healing towards you, encouraging emotional support for you and your endeavors. You instinctively understand others emotional needs putting you in favor with them, making relationships with women especially harmonious.

Chiron Square Moon

There may be issues with you and your mother, or she may have been ill or been absent at times which inhibited your relationship with her. This has made opening up emotionally to others very challenging and difficult for you. The challenge is expressing your true feelings, even if it is anger. Turning this anger into courage is the positive expression you are really challenged with doing.

Chiron Trine Moon

You truly understand what makes people tick, as you can see their emotional makeup very quickly. You sense what people need to feel secure, and you make them feel at ease in your presence. You are a natural care giver, and nurturer. Healers, nurses, child care providers could have this aspect strong in their chart. This aspect indicates your mother was a healing influence and a strong mentor to you and your upbringing.

Chiron Opposition Moon

There may have been a distance from your mother so that you may have not received the nurturing and care giving you needed. She may have been working, or very busy with other family duties, chores etc. This created a distance and a wound emotionally in relating to others, especially women. Many with this difficult aspect have eating issues, too much, not enough, emotional eating etc. Disorders such as anorexia or obesity can be a challenge.

Chiron Conjunction Mercury

You are a strong communicator, and have the ability to be a teacher, shaman, doctor, and healer to many. You seem to understand the healing power of thought forms, and words. Astrology may appeal to you as a language of symbols and archetypes. You would also do well with computer programming or coding.

Chiron Sextile Mercury

You have a strong sense of communicating what needs to be said, as you see clearly the base cause of situations. You like getting to the bottom of the issue, and have the mental capacity for this kind of work. Healing, educating, communicating and mentoring others is a strong suit you have. The language of symbols also calls to you whether it's computer language or astrology, and using symbols and archetypes as meanings. If you have siblings you would get along well with them, and may be a teacher for them, or them to you.

Chiron Square Mercury

Take care not to be too harsh with your words as you know firsthand that they can heal or harm, and you would be better off being the healer. You may have been wounded by the words of others, criticized, or made fun of due to some non-important issue that has been overblown. You may have had a speech impediment or an issue with reading early on and the stigma took a long time to heal. Your awareness of this brings you to healing with words, counseling, hypnotherapy, and the like would be great for you to explore.

Chiron Trine Mercury

Your words have a strong impact on others, and you seem to be the key that opens up the proper channels of communication with others. You find talking to others is something you enjoy, and would be great at public speaking as your words bring inspiration to others. Subjects that solve issues interest you, research, mysticism, philosophy, healing, actually you have a well rounded range of topics.

Chiron Opposition Mercury

The opposition of Chiron and Mercury shows you can shut down if what you're hearing strikes a nerve in you. Most likely something from the past that was said to you still is a raw and open wound. This opposition may open it up again, but it is the opportunity for you to take a deep look inside and do some inner healing. Think of those who trigger this in you to be your teacher or mentor in disguise.

Chiron Conjunction Venus

This aspect shows a deep wound in your love life. This started out most likely in your early years as you feel that you were different or not accepted by one or both of your parents. There may have been a real or perceived feeling of rejection. The challenge for you is to realize that nothing is wrong with you in any way, and it is time to value yourself. Take some time to explore making yourself look better and feel better by getting new clothes, a new haircut or a make over in some way. Not because of others but because you know you deserve this.

Chiron Sextile Venus

You have a gift for healing others through beauty, art, or design. This can manifest in many ways such as being a hairdresser or barber, and seeing people feel better about their themselves, as you make them look better. Or a landscaper who creates a beautiful yard that makes you feel like you are in paradise or heaven. This is transforming and healing. How do you utilize this aspect in your own life? Others feel very comforted in your presence.

Chiron Square Venus

Often people with this aspect have a wound about their appearance, feelings of not being good enough, self-esteem issues. They may have never been told they were loved enough or that they were handsome or pretty, resulting in a deep inferiority complex. This can be also caused by a betrayal in early life that raises trust issues with partners in the current time frame. These issues need to be healed in order to have a fulfilling relationship with another, but first we need to have a fulfilling, loving relationship with ourselves.

Chiron Trine Venus

This trine aspect can bring out deep felt emotions that can be used artistically or musically. Songs about unrequited love, tragedy, loss and betrayal can be expressed through beautiful lyrics, or a love story well written. You may have your own Cinderella story or Prince Charming story or two that brings up these deep-felt feelings. Healing through your love life can be a manifestation of this aspect or even marrying a healer, or doctor.

Chiron Opposition Venus

Relationships can seem hard with this aspect, it can bring the search for the soul mate to help heal your inner wounds. Your wounds revolve around feeling loved, wanted and needed, so the search for someone to fill those shoes is a difficult task. Unrequited love, triangulations, entanglements, or falling for those who are unavailable can be problematic for you. Do some healing work on yourself, improving your self-esteem, image, get a make over, treat yourself and love yourself, and you will attract the right person for you.

Chiron Conjunction Mars

This aspect can be challenging and how you use this energy for good or bad is the key. Many have a quest to become a hero or heroine, with this aspect. Challenging sports competition can be a key release for healing inner wounds. This can manifest in sexual conquests and challenges as well, as in "another notch on the bed post". What is going on under the surface is expressing the Mars energy in a therapeutic and healing way that is the goal. If you repress your anger there can be manipulation and passive aggressive tendencies causing others to lash out at you, then you are the victim. Review childhood messages of power and control to see where this issue (energy) comes from. Once realized this is a very powerful placement and use of energy in positive ways.

Chiron Sextile Mars

You have a knack for getting challenging tasks done with ease. You make difficult situations turn out for the better, and utilize the stress of the situation to make the situation turn out okay. Yoga is a very good outlet for you and highly recommended. You would excel in sports as well.

Chiron Square Mars

You do well under pressure and in emergency type situations. Fields such as emergency medical response work would appeal to you, such as paramedics, police work, rescue work on all types. You like the challenge and want to help. There may have been deep anger issues in childhood that need to be resolved, conflicts with parents and authorities for example. The challenge is how to constructively utilize this energy.

Chiron Trine Mars

You may be attracted to careers in healing, such as a surgeon, or emergency medical technician, acupuncture would be good as well. Sports are another great outlet for you, even if it's jogging. You have a natural skill at doing well in the competitive areas.

Chiron Opposition Mars

You may attract relationships that can be combative, and need healing. You may have to learn to stand in your own power and take the appropriate action that leads to inspiring others. This may be very difficult and cause many battles. You need to honor yourself and the rights of others as well. This can be a tricky aspect to have. You may have to help others discover their inner drive and potential, and guide them to have the strength to move forward.

Chiron Conjunction Jupiter

There may be a great quest to seek the truth, as a result of being misled or lied to at an early age. Religion, philosophy of life and meaning may be the endless search for those with this aspect. Belief in Santa Clause and being let down may lead to a loss of faith in what is told to us, therefore not believing anything created a wound deeply needing to be healed. Healing quickly from illnesses is another manifestation of Jupiter conjunction Chiron. This aspect also makes the best out of difficult situations. Lessons always seem to be learned from the experiences and adventures in life.

Chiron Sextile Jupiter

This aspect gives you an excellent ability to mentor, teach, coach and train. Higher learning from a master, one who has done the research and walked the walk and is now going to be able to talk the talk and spread the word – this person is you. You love learning and just as much – sharing this knowledge and teaching.

Chiron Square Jupiter

There may be wounds that caused lack of faith or belief in a higher power or "the system". Either way you have doubts and are skeptical of healing treatments, doctors, and authority, including God. There may be serious reasons and situations that caused you to be this way, but reflecting on the reasons that you believe what you believe is a key to understanding how to heal this skepticism, and lack of trust and faith. The challenge may be an endless quest to find the truth, God, enlightenment, in many different ways. Sometimes life will bring you this "proof" through adverse life situations that turn out to be blessings.

Chiron Trine Jupiter

You have a great gift of inspiring and helping others find their truths in life. You would make a great mentor, and teacher with this combination. You love higher knowledge and education and learn easily. You could have a great interest in healing, and becoming a doctor of some type, this would work well for you. You will reach many people on a large scale.

Chiron Opposition Jupiter

Many disappointing events shaped your belief or disbelief in the opportunities in life and the goodness of humanity. This can be from unrealized or broken dreams and promises not kept by parents or elders. Relationships are where you look to find the answers, through other people's beliefs and life events that turned out well, giving you hope and optimism. Sometimes seeing the misfortunes of others keeps us in check about how lucky we really are.

Chiron Conjunction Saturn

You may have authority issues, most likely from parents, especially the father figure. This may cause you to take responsibilities to the extreme one way or the other. Either you take on responsibility for everyone including yourself or taking no responsibility even for your own self. It is usually the extreme one way. Once this wound is healed you can become a great authority figure to others, a leader.

Chiron Sextile Saturn

Your path to success has had many painstaking challenges, and you have passed them all, and learned from them, therefore you are given many opportunities even at a young age that others may not have. Success in management, and teaching, mentoring and coaching are all suggested with this positive placement.

Chiron Square Saturn

Many serious challenges and disciplines have been placed in your path. They were all very serious karmic lessons, that you survived and conquered. What did you learn from these experiences and how did you grow as a result? That is what should be asked and looked at in a positive growing experience type way.

Chiron Trine Saturn

You have a natural talent for being a shaman, healer, teacher, mentor and coach. You have the discipline needed to organize and train people due to your past conditioning and skills. Chiron is a healer, teacher, shaman, mystic in many areas he was also a master astrologer. You can develop with great skill in any of these areas.

Chiron Opposition Saturn

Many conflicts and challenges with partnerships and authority figures was most likely the case early on in life. Hopefully you've learned to understand self-responsibility and responsibility for your own well-being. That was the major lesson which could take at least 30 years to figure out. Reflect back on your relationship with your parents are those issues now playing a part in your intimate relationships? If so you need to re-examine what the real issues were so you can heal current relationship issues.

Chiron Conjunction Uranus

This aspect makes our uniqueness our wound. Being "different" is hard, "different is lonely". We can be outcast and seem like aliens on planet earth. But this unique individuality is what you need to heal and become, and that is your life mission. It may be that you work in technology as a radiologist, or whatever unique career you desire, go for it. This aspect also favors astrology, you may be strongly attracted to it and become a great astrologer yourself.

Chiron Sextile Uranus

You can communicate in symbols, this makes you talented in computer systems and languages as well as the language of astrology, and you would do well and learn them both. Technology is second nature to you, something you can use to your advantage. Interest in healing with the latest technology may strongly interest you.

Chiron Square Uranus

You may feel like a square peg in a round hole, as you don't fit in too easily with the public at large. Embrace this as it can be the thing that brings you notoriety and gives you your uniqueness. Relationships can be challenging given you need your freedom and don't like being restrained in any way. Find someone who is as unconventional as you are, and who isn't clingy. There is someone like you out there for you. Don't set your relationship standards by the standards of society, yours are unique and you are the only one who controls your standards.

Chiron Trine Uranus

You have a brilliant and original thinking mind. You have a knack for taking old and outworn ideas and creating something new and innovative out of them. You are a natural inventor and creator. Areas such as technology, computers, science and astrology are favored with this aspect.

Chiron Opposition Uranus

You may have difficulty with relationships until you realize that you just need your freedom. You don't like convention, and "alternative" is a key word for you in this life, as you have an alternative to most everything. Structure is hard for you, if it's too rigid you will rebel and break away. Therefore authority is something you feel challenged by. You may feel like a maverick and that is truly what you are. Once you come to terms with this, your relationships, both personal and impersonal, will improve greatly.

Chiron Conjunction Neptune

You naturally feel the emotions of people around you. This is called being an empath, its also a newer term for psychic, a specific psychic ability to feel the emotions of those around you. This can act as a debilitating awareness that is feared, but it can also be a great skill to help heal yourself and others around you. You need to learn the art of psychic protection, to help you discern your true feelings from others, and to be able to shield when you need to. You are a natural healer, embrace this and you will be much happier.

Chiron Sextile Neptune

Creativity is a natural state for you as you have a great imagination that goes beyond everyday awareness. You notice all the subtle energies around you and are stimulated favorably by them. You tap into others energies and the energies around you in the room, or building etc. You may not even be consciously aware of this. You are a natural psychic in a sense, and the more you use your right brain, the creative side, the more you stimulate this awareness. Music, dance, art, colors, are all great tools for you to utilize your natural talents. These talents are healing both for yourself and others.

Chiron Square Neptune

Boundaries have been an issue for you since childhood. You know more about others than they tell you, and you go beyond normal awareness and pick up the rest of the story psychically. This aspect can have the negative effects of Neptune challenging you; boundary issues with self and others, alcohol and drugs, addiction of any kind, fear and betrayal. The challenge is to look at all of this squarely and honestly and make the positive changes needed, that will greatly improve your life. You can be a natural psychic or healer and can help many. Energy work is favored, such as reiki, for instance.

Chiron Trine Neptune

You are a very creative and inspired individual with many great healing talents, even psychic abilities. Energy work in healing is favored, such as reiki. These techniques are good for you and would be good to learn to help yourself and others. Naturally you're highly psychic with this aspect especially in areas of healing. It would be wise to learn more about psychic development, prayer and meditation. Creative outlets are also very healing, music, dance, art, singing are some outlets suggested for you.

Chiron Opposition Neptune

Trust is something you must learn in your life. This aspect shows you may lack trust as you have been betrayed many times and therefore have strong boundary issues. The true test is to learn to "trust yourself" and your own intuition and inner knowing. This is a big wound to heal in yourself but by doing so will improve your relationships greatly. If you get the warning that you should not trust someone learn to listen to that voice and change the outcome so you are not betrayed again.

Chiron Conjunction Pluto

You may have major control issues, as a result of someone in your early childhood who had extreme control over you. Sometimes there was an abuse of power that went along with the control. As a result you can become extremely controlling of situations or others so you don't feel "'controlled". This however will backfire and people will either back away from you or resent you and try to get even. Its best if you go deep within and forgive and let go or "forget". Then realize that the universe works with you when you surrender your power and control and there will be no need to ever fear control again.

Chiron Sextile Pluto

You have deep insight into the motivations and behaviors of others. This may give you interest in psychology, criminology, and forensics. Why people do what they do is fascinating to you. You are a natural at healing, the modalities good for you are hypnosis, transactional analysis, trance work and mediumship, grief counselor.

Chiron Square Pluto

There is a challenge in dealing with others; you have control issues which were caused from early childhood. Your parents may have been overly controlling. You may feel you have to control everything and all situations around you. The sooner you learn to surrender your power the universe will respond and you will actually be a force for the higher good. Learning the law of attraction will greatly improve your happiness and life. You are natural at manifesting, you just need to learn the way to do it with no resistance.

Chiron Trine Pluto

Healing and transformational work will be a natural for you. Modalities such as hypnosis, transactional analysis, grief work would be good for you to do and you would do well to master these techniques for healing others. You are also a great motivator and inspiration to the masses as you accomplish your goals you show the world what you have done this insures them that they can too. This aspect also favors work in medical and scientific fields.

Chiron Opposition Pluto

Relationships may be in need of healing for you. You attract powerful individuals who try to dominate or control you, creating the deep need for you to heal your inner wounds. There may be power and control issues bouncing back and forth with your partner until you heal this deep-seated condition from childhood. Read books on the law of attraction to help let go of the need to feel in control.

Chiron Conjunction MC

You most likely will be in one of the following professions: teaching, mentoring, counseling, astrology, medical field, all of which are Chiron ruled. Your father or dominant parent may have done the same type of work or inspired you to do your career of choice. You may be known as the "Wounded healer".

Chiron Sextile MC

You may receive group support and recognition in your work, financial aid or favorable monetary conditions will reflect in your career. You find your knowledge and skills payoff well in the long run, you have a perfect reputation and are well known for your field of work. People seek you out for your knowledge, healing abilities and your expertise.

Chiron Square MC

There may be challenges to overcome with regard to your work and career life. Relationships can be challenging with your significant other or your business partners. Perhaps there is an open wound that needs to be healed in order to move forward on the job or up the ladder. Showing others that you're ready and capable is the key.

Chiron Trine MC

You have many special skills and talents, they are easily shown and rewarded through your career and standing in life. You just have to make sure to utilize your special talents and skills, and not waste them, that is the challenge. You may possess some healing ability or knowledge, that will be utilized in your work life.

Chiron Opposition MC

The home life may have been very challenging and difficult in your early childhood. Perhaps you had to take care of others in the family especially if there was a "wound" of some kind that effected the family. It may be that your family was dysfunctional and you had to try to fix the problem. These early experiences have shaped you and made you stronger inside, more secure with yourself. These experiences also shaped you for a career in helping others in some way. You would succeed in a career that involves healing, teaching, training coaching, counseling, and mentoring.

Chiron Conjunction ASC

You may have felt like you were from a different planet as a child, much too wise, and you may not have fit in with the rest of the crowd. This may have made you introverted and self-reflective. Many with this aspect felt rejected at an early age. You have a natural thirst for knowledge and love to read. Once you start to feel comfortable being you, then you become a natural teacher, trainer, coach and mentor, or even a shaman. Science, philosophy, and healing are interests and skills of yours. You will likely be a teacher on some level, a master at something, teaching future masters. Astrology most likely is an interest of yours.

Chiron Sextile ASC

This aspect gives you a maverick personality, one who follows his own path in life. You may not be a rebel it's just that you have your own agenda and don't want to follow the crowd blindly. You may be considered a shaman a teacher, mentor and a mediator to many.

Chiron Square ASC

You may have had conflicting beliefs taught to you as a child, and questioned your teachers and the teachings of your elders. This can cause conflict within yourself, and your family. You may go on a spiritual quest at some point to find the truth. This may lead you to a path that resonates with your true beliefs and philosophies. In this you become the teacher, and mentor to many. There may have been a physical or mental wound you had to go through that teaches you and inspires you to become an advocate for that exact cause. This was a life lesson and goal you had before incarnation.

Chiron Trine ASC

You have a gift for inspiring others, through your own life experiences (in this or past lives). Many would say you're an old soul, wise beyond your years. You are a natural teacher, and mentor. Many of your teachings come from your own lessons in the past of "hard knocks". Astrology, science, music and healing are all interests you would do well to explore.

Chiron Opposition ASC

You will attract partners that may be in the healing professions such as doctors, counselors, shamans, energy workers and healers. The partner may have an inner wound that seemingly is impossible to heal, that they have to learn to adapt and live with. This may turn out that they become the advocate for the disease or condition that they have had to bear for a lifetime. Your partner may be a mentor to you, healing your own inner deep wounds physically or psychologically.

www.ingramcontent.com/pod-product-compliance
Lightning Source LLC
Chambersburg PA
CBHW050553160426
43199CB00015B/2644